Beyond Window-Dressing?
Canadian Children's Fantasy at the Millennium

K.V. Johansen

Other books by K.V. Johansen

The Cassandra Virus
The Drone War
The Serpent Bride: Stories From Medieval Danish Ballads
Nightwalker: The Warlocks of Talverdin I
Treason in Eswy: The Warlocks of Talverdin II
Warden of Greyrock: The Warlocks of Talverdin III

The Torrie Quests novels
Torrie and the Dragon
Torrie and the Pirate-Queen
Torrie and the Firebird
Torrie and the Snake-Prince

Pippin and Mabel picture books
Pippin Takes a Bath
Pippin and the Bones
Pippin and Pudding

Non-fiction
Quests and Kingdoms:
A Grown-Up's Guide to Children's Fantasy Literature

BEYOND WINDOW-DRESSING?
Canadian Children's Fantasy at the Millennium

K.V. Johansen

SYBERTOOTH INC
SACKVILLE, NEW BRUNSWICK

Litteris Elegantis Madefimus

For the nieces, nephews, godsons, et cetera.
Rene, David, Ashley, Ben, Rachel,
Gabriel, Julian, Fabien, Tristan ...
so far.

Copyright © 2007 K.V. Johansen
Cover art copyright © 2007 Sybertooth Inc.
Cover by Artemisia

First published 2007 by   Sybertooth Inc.
59 Salem St.
Sackville, NB
E4L 4J6
Canada
www.sybertooth.ca

Paper is acid free and meets all ANSI standards for archival quality.

Library and Archives Canada Cataloguing in Publication

Johansen, K. V. (Krista V.), 1968-
Beyond window dressing? : Canadian children's fantasy at the millennium / K.V. Johansen.

Includes bibliographical references and index.
ISBN 978-0-9688024-5-8

1. Fantasy fiction, Canadian (English)--History and criticism.
2. Children's literature, Canadian (English)--History and criticism.
I. Title.

PS8069.J64 2007   C813'.08766099282   C2007-906221-0

TABLE OF CONTENTS

Foreword	7
I: Beyond the Brownies	10
II: Time-Travel	31
III: Magic in the Primary World	41
IV: Speculative Fantasy	60
V: Re-imaginings of Older Tales	70
VI: Historical Fantasy	78
VII: Animal Fantasy	84
VIII: Dual-World Fantasy	88
IX: Secondary and Alternate World Fantasy	102
X: Beyond Window-Dressing	124
Bibliography	130
Index	139

Acknowledgements

Beyond Window-Dressing? began its life as a paper written through the generosity of the Canadian section of the International Board on Books for Young People, from whom I received the 2004 Frances E. Russell Award. Although *Window-Dressing* rapidly expanded into something rather larger than a paper, the Frances E. Russell Award and IBBY Canada remain its godparents, to which and whom I extend my sincere thanks. The New Brunswick Public Library system and its interlibrary loans service was also an indispensable part of this project, as was the Eileen Wallace Children's Literature Collection at the University of New Brunswick. Dr. Tristanne Connolly of St. Jerome's University, Waterloo, aided the research and commented on drafts of the manuscript. Parts of the discussion of some books may have appeared earlier in slightly different form as reviews in *Resource Links*, or in a few cases may be adapted from the lengthier commentaries on particular authors previously published in *Quests and Kingdoms*.

The sophisticated mind...may refuse to admit that there can be anything in ogres or dragons, since it believes that such things have in our day long been relegated to the nursery (whence they are now being cast forth onto the rubbish heap). O Impoverished day! But it is not the first time that valuable things have been cast upon the rubbish heap at the bidding of fashion—to be painfully sought for again later.

J.R.R. Tolkien
Beowulf and the Critics [1]

FOREWORD

COMPARED TO OTHER GENRES of children's literature in Canada, fantasy got off to a very slow start. Canadian children have always had access to British and American books, but despite the availability of imported literature, there was throughout the twentieth century a thriving body of Canadian writers at work in some other genres, particularly realistic adventure, nature stories, historical, and "problem" novels. Fantasy remained a very minor part of Canadian children's literature. In Carpenter's and Prichard's *The Oxford Companion to Children's Literature*, the authors' comment on the quality of Canadian historical fiction novels for children, that "...until recently most were educational rather than imaginative...",[2] applies to fantasy as well, to the extent that it existed at all. It was the late eighties and nineties before much fantasy appeared in which the story tried to stand on its own merits as fantasy. In most, the fantasy was either the trimming on a story that itself obviously existed to serve as a vehicle for some theme, a story that was "about" death, alienation, or divorce first and foremost, rather than a story that contained these themes as a natural part of its unfolding, or it was a mere veneer of novelty tacked on top of the plot, a "twist" in a story that belonged to some other

---

[1] Tolkien, *Beowulf and the Critics*, p. 108.
[2] Carpenter and Prichard, *The Oxford Companion to Children's Literature*, p. 94.

genre. At the end of the twentieth century, fantasy for children and teens remained the exception in Canadian publishers' catalogues, and often, the fantastic presented was a supernatural, paranormal, or occult element in a book for teens which, if published more or less unchanged for adults, would be classed as horror, romance, or "family saga". Even into the nineties, unabashed fantasy such as O.R. Melling's *The Druid's Tune* (1983) or Alison Baird's *The Dragon's Egg* (1994) was rare; rarer still were works as convincing in literary reality and as well-written as these two examples. Through most of the twentieth century, outright secondary world fantasy, or even fantasy in which magic entered the familiar world, hardly appeared at all in Canadian books. When it did, rarely could it bear comparison to the best in Britain and the United States; like the American adult fantasy of the seventies, it often appeared thin, poorly conceived, or derivative.

Then, around the turn of the twenty-first century, several years after the appearance of the first of J.K. Rowling's novels, Canadian publishers woke up to the existence and popularity of *Harry Potter*. At a time when British and American publishers were rushing their fantasy backlists out in new covers and reissuing all the out-of-print fantasy they could find from about 1960 onwards (to the great joy of those attempting to find beloved library books of their childhood), Canadian publishers finally stopped telling authors, "Fantasy doesn't sell; children don't read fantasy," and began publishing it. This study examines the development of Canadian children's fantasy in the five-year period from 2000 to 2004.

In *Today's Parent*, a representative of the Halifax children's bookstore Woozles is quoted as saying that fantasy, prior to 1997 (when *Harry Potter and the Philosopher's Stone* was published), did not sell: "Now easily 50 percent of our fiction is good-quality fantasy, thanks to Harry Potter."[3] The "fifty percent" quoted by Woozles is for fantasy in general, not Canadian fantasy, but this recognition that the genre has an audience and is thus potentially

---

[3]Susan MacLeod. "Life as a Parent: The top twenty breakthroughs: How life has changed in the last twenty years". *Today's Parent*, October 2004.
http://www.todaysparent.com/lifeasparent/parenting/article.jsp?content=20040907_154326_5240&page=1 — accessed July 11, 2005.

profitable, even in Canada, can be presumed to be the reason works of fantasy are now considered for publication by most Canadian children's publishers, rather than by only the exceptional and daring few. However, the question of whether the fantasy now being published in Canada is good fantasy, capable of withstanding comparison to the best of Britain or the United States, has not been paid much attention. If a cross-section of fantasy published in Canada during the first five years of the twenty-first century is examined, will it show that Canadian fantasy has matured beyond clumsy allegory, moral instruction, and that favourite Canadian genre, "time-travel to learn history", or will it reveal that the fantastic must still perform heavy labour to justify its presence on Canadian school and library shelves, that fantasy elements are most acceptable when limited to a derivative window-dressing?

I
BEYOND THE BROWNIES

IN *MODERN CANADIAN CHILDREN'S BOOKS*, her 1987 survey of Canadian children's literature published between 1975 and 1985, Judith Saltman observes that "True fantasy, however—classic epic fantasy of serious moral struggle between good and evil, set in fully realized Other Worlds—has never been a strength in Canadian writing for children".[1] By "True fantasy...set in fully realized Other Worlds" Saltman refers to secondary world fantasy.[2] The insistence on the conflict of absolutes, the struggle between good and evil, as an essential aspect of it ignores the broad range of worlds, cosmologies, and plots found in secondary world fantasy, but her observation contains a valid point: there had been little noteworthy secondary world fantasy written and published in Canada during that decade. Saltman attributes the Canadian weakness in "true fantasy" to Canada's "overpowering and alienating landscape" and lack of "history rooted in humanly hospitable places",[3] observing that native myths and legends have failed to resonate with the "national imagination"[4] as the history and landscape of Britain has with British writers. On the subject of using aboriginal myth and legend, she justly points out the failure of Canadian authors to write anything approaching Australian Patricia Wrightson's *The Book of Wirrun* trilogy (published 1977-1981), which features a contemporary Australian aboriginal teen as hero and vividly peoples the Australian landscape with the supernatural of aboriginal myth and legend.

Saltman finds that time-travel is the "most vigorous sub-

---

[1] *Modern Canadian Children's Books*, p. 81.
[2] The definition of "sub-creation" in the *Oxford English Dictionary Online* is "J. R. R. Tolkien's word for the process of inventing an imaginary or secondary world, different from the primary world but internally consistent." Secondary world fantasy is literature set in such an imaginary world.
[3] *Modern Canadian Children's Books*, p. 81.
[4] *ibid.*, p. 82.

genre" of children's fantasy in Canada.[5] Her chapter on fantasy discusses, if science fiction and retellings of fairy-tales and fables are excluded, works by some sixteen authors published during the decade her book covers. Of these, most are categorised as "time travel fantasy" or "supernatural and psychological fantasy", with only *Jacob Two-Two Meets the Hooded Fang* discussed as "light fantasy". Not one is secondary world fantasy. With the exception of O.R. Melling's *The Druid's Tune* (1983; 1984 Canadian Library Association Young Adult Book Award), those categorised as "time travel" are stories which illustrate aspects of regional or family history for the benefit of the protagonists.

In contrast, Melling's novel uses Maeve of Connaught's invasion of Ulster, from the Irish epic the *Táin bó Cuailnge*, as the backdrop to a story about Canadian teens in Ireland who are inadvertently drawn into a legendary rather than an historical past by their uncle's hired man, who is an aspect of the fragmented druid Peadar. Jimmy and Rosemary are caught up in warfare between Queen Maeve and Cuchulainn, champion of Ulster. They experience the complex, frequently tragic loyalties and rivalries of a tribal, heroic society. They are initially allied to opposing sides; Rosemary falls in love with Maeve's son Maine, but is nearly sacrificed by the queen and barely escapes murder at the battle-mad Cuchulainn's hands, while Jimmy becomes Cuchulainn's friend and charioteer. Eventually they take part in a battle in support of Cuchulainn, though they work hard to avoid killing. Both are alternately entranced and repulsed by the heroic ethos of the age. The druid Peadar's barely-comprehended quest to reunify himself is at the core of the plot. Although Rosemary and Jimmy learn a great deal about themselves and have their attitudes to the world changed as well, the story never becomes the slave of a history lesson.

The books classed by Saltman as "supernatural or psychological" are all ones with relatively contemporary real world settings into which some aspect of the supernatural—black magic, folkloric ghosts, reincarnation, psychic powers—intrudes. Among the "supernatural or psychological", only in two, Welwyn Wilton Katz's *Witchery Hill* (1984) and Donn Kushner's lyrical, funny,

---

[5] *ibid.*, p. 84.

and moving *Uncle Jacob's Ghost Story* (1984) is the fantastic element the foundation of the plot. (In the former, it is the desire of a coven of witches to possess the knowledge in an evil book, and in the latter, an immigrant's reunion with the ghosts of two beloved friends of his youth.) In all the others, the supernatural element is the means of exploring the author's theme; it can be metaphor or allegory for a psychological process, or a device to illustrate a particular idea. Fantasy is subordinate to the purpose of the story or is imposed on the story; it is window-dressing, not integral to or inherent in the story.

In her seminal work on Canadian children's literature, *The Republic of Childhood* (published 1967), Sheila Egoff discussed the books of eleven Canadian fantasy writers (if retellings of folk- and fairy-tales are excluded), but found many of those of little enduring merit: "Once again a chapter must end with the now-familiar complaint about the relative dearth of imaginative literature",[6] and "Canadian children will have to continue to look to England and the United States for the books that stir and do not merely tell."[7] By 1990, when *The New Republic of Childhood* (by Egoff and Judith Saltman) appeared, the number of authors included has risen to twenty-nine (leaving aside a few examples of animal-fantasy in which the only fantastic element lies in talking animals). Egoff and Saltman summarize their discussion of fantasy by describing Canadian authors as "better realists than fantasists, creating their most memorable scenes in full reality".[8] They do ultimately and optimistically conclude that "the scope of the genre has widened considerably" and that Canadian fantasy is "in step with fantasies from other English-speaking countries" due to "emphasis on characterization and overall sophistication".[9]

However, Egoff and Saltman have earlier criticised as falling short nearly all their examples of fantasy that moves imaginatively beyond children's ordinary and everyday lives. They find that the complexity and mythological backgrounding of such works creates a situation where, in their words, "credibility and emotional

---

[6] *The Republic of Childhood*, p. 156.
[7] *ibid.*, p. 157.
[8] *The New Republic of Childhood*, p. 271.
[9] *ibid.*, p. 272.

involvement are imperilled".[10] They fault as undisciplined those few writers, such as Melling, Katz, and Michael Bedard, whom they do describe as writing books with plots more complex than the encounters of everyday children with magic talismans or time-travel with historical or familial function. Fantasy which is memorable mostly for scenes "in full reality" (that is, in the primary world—they do not mean the feeling of reality created by serious attention to the art of sub-creation[11]), does lack something required to be "in step" with British or American fantasy, despite the authors' implication that Canadian writers' "contemporaries in other countries" are also better at realism.[12] Their argument creates the impression that what is most valuable in fantasy is its novelty when attached to an otherwise realistic story of the primary world; "full reality" is what matters, not the ability of the fantasy, and the book as a whole, to induce literary belief[13] or to create a credible reality far removed from the everyday life of the audience. Egoff and Saltman characterise "All the best fantasies of the past" as having "simple plots" and state that "In Canadian fantasy, too, the simpler fantasies work best and certainly carry the most conviction",[14] which again devalues those fantasies which reach beyond the ordinary and everyday to portray larger worlds and ideas more complex than coming to understand one's grandmother by time-travel, dealing with bullies, or settling into the New World. Not only was most Canadian fantasy thin, but the critical culture within Canada praised it for its thinness.

In contrast to this, however, Saltman's 1996 article "The development of Canadian fantasy literature for children",[15] updates the survey in her own book and in *The New Republic of Childhood*, including later works by Welwyn Wilton Katz, Michael Bedard, and O.R. Melling. Her conclusion in this article is that these authors demonstrate "an ability to work with ambitious and com-

---

[10] *ibid.*, p. 271.
[11] I.e. in a secondary world created by what Tolkien termed a "sub-creator". ("On Fairy-Stories". *The Monsters and the Critics and Other Essays.* p. 132.)
[12] *ibid.*, p. 271.
[13] The phrase is Tolkien's: literary belief on the part of the reader is the result of successful sub-creation on the part of the storyteller. ("On Fairy-Stories". *The Monsters and the Critics and Other Essays.* p. 132.)
[14] *The New Republic of Childhood*, p. 271.
[15] *Canadian Children's Literature* 82, vol. 22:2, 1996. pp. 69-79.

plex subjects",[16] suggesting a reassessment either of the works in question, or of what makes good fantasy. Either way, it indicates an optimism on Saltman's part about the development of less simplistic fantasy in Canada.

In a much larger work examining children's fantasy within an international context, Egoff found only six Canadian authors worthy of mention. Those Canadian works included in *Worlds Within: Children's Fantasy from the Middle Ages to Today* (1988) range from the light whimsy of Cox's *Brownies* to the psychological, family-relationship-driven *Julie* of Cora Taylor, with its psychic protagonist. Several are time-travel stories by Janet Lunn and Kit Pearson, while those of Catherine Anthony Clark mythologize the British Columbia wilderness. Ruth Nichols is the only author included who attempts to portray another world. However, compared to the fantasy being published in Britain and the United States by contemporaries of these writers, the works Egoff chose to include, when actually read rather than taken in digest, generally fall short in depth and richness of sub-creation.

The earliest Canadian fantasy to be discussed by Egoff in *Worlds Within*, and the first Canadian-written fantasy to have an international impact, was Palmer Cox's *Brownies*, inspired by the mischievous, helpful fairies from Scottish folklore. Cox was an illustrator and cartoonist; his stories are told in rhymed couplets with big, busy pictures, the details of which contain numerous comic subplots. The *Brownies* stories were written and set in the United States, and published there and in Great Britain. Cox ultimately retired back to Canada and built a grand house in Granby, Québec, called Brownie Castle, evidence of his success. Cox's Brownies spend their time exploring the world, taking an uninhibited delight in their environment. They perform good deeds, such as rescuing beached whales and harvesting apples, but mostly they have fun while experiencing the world as children might: tobogganing, canoeing, and so on. The stories were also meant to be educational, so they contain discourses on subjects such as Niagara Falls or the American states. The Brownies became icons and were one of the first graphic images to become a marketing phenomenon—the Brownie camera, one of the first

---

[16] *ibid.*, p. 78.

cheap, easy-to-use cameras, was named after them. The *Brownies* stories were initially published in the American children's magazines *Wide Awake* and *St. Nicholas*, and *The Brownies: Their Book*, the first of around a dozen collections, came out in 1887. By the time the first of the *Brownies* books was published, however, numerous classics of children's fantasy were already in existence (and this is excluding folktale collections, such as those of Jakob and Wilhelm Grimm): H.C. Andersen's "The Little Mermaid" (1837) and "The Snow Queen" (1846); John Ruskin's *The King of the Golden River* (1851); William Makepeace Thackeray's *The Rose and the Ring* (1855); Charles Kingsley's *The Water-Babies: A Fairy-Tale For a Land-Baby* (1863); Lewis Carroll's *Alice's Adventures in Wonderland* (1865) and *Through the Looking-Glass and What Alice Found There* (1872); and George MacDonald's *At the Back of the North Wind* (serialized 1868/book form 1871), *The Princess and the Goblin* (1870/1872) and *The Princess and Curdie* (1877/1883). *The Brownies*, compared to these, is lightweight stuff.

In the years that followed the first appearance of the Brownies in book form, fantasy continued to be very prominent among stories published for children, particularly in Great Britain. Andrew Lang's *Fairy Books* began to appear with *The Blue Fairy Book* in 1889 and ended with *Lilac* in 1910, retelling the folk- and fairy-tales of the world for English-speaking children and influencing the imaginations of a generation. Much other fantasy still loved today was published during subsequent decades: American L. Frank Baum's *The Wonderful Wizard of Oz* (1900) and its many sequels; E. Nesbit's *Five Children and It* (1902), the first of a number of fantasies she wrote between 1902 and 1913's *Wet Magic*; J.M. Barrie's *Peter and Wendy* (1911—a book that went through several versions and titles and was originally a play, *Peter Pan*, in 1904); Kipling's *Puck of Pook's Hill* (1906) and *Rewards and Fairies* (1910); Kenneth Grahame's *The Wind in the Willows* (1908); Walter de la Mare's *The Three Mulla-Mulgars* (1910); John Masefield's *The Midnight Folk* (1927) and *The Box of Delights* (1935); P.L. Travers' *Mary Poppins* (1934); and most importantly, Tolkien's *The Hobbit* (1937). However, no Canadian author appears again in Egoff's *Worlds Within* until the nineteen-fifties, and Catherine Anthony Clark.[17]

There are six books by Clark, written between 1950 and 1966. The earliest of these is *The Golden Pine Cone* (1950), in which siblings Bren and Lucy find a golden pine cone, which is an earring stolen by the Indian giant Nasookin from Tekontha, the ruler of the land. Bren and Lucy set off to return it to her, accompanied by their husky Ooshka, who offers advice along the way. The main plot, though is their quest to help Princess Onomara, Nasookin's exiled lover, get her heart back so that she will be able to love the giant again, which will stop him threatening others with his magic; this accomplished, the children return home.

In all of her books, Clark tried to make a Canadian landscape and mythology the foundation of the fantastic in the story. She did not succeed the way Australia's Patricia Wrightson did for Australia a decade later with her *Book of Wirrun* trilogy (1977-1981). Clark's writing is simply not of the same calibre as Wrightson's. Clark's characters are characterless children who trot through their adventures without undergoing any great trials, any real testing or change. Her plots are formulaic: the books are set in British Columbia's interior in the fifties and sixties, the main characters are usually siblings whose personalities can be summed up as the Boy and the Girl; they encounter magical beings who are either spirits in the form of natives, or creatures from traditional west-coast mythology, or invented creatures of the British Columbian landscape. The children are drawn into this supernatural world by a chance encounter, have an adventure with no real danger or cost to themselves, resolve the problems they meet, and return home. They do not come home changed or wiser; the lessons are not learned, but are demonstrated solely for the reader's benefit. But Clark tried, as no-one else had tried, to make a truly Canadian supernatural. *The Sun Horse* (Macmillan Canada 1951), even received the 1952 CLA Book of the Year for Children Award. As fantasy, Clark's stories fall into a category somewhere between the

---

[17] Although *The Magic Walking Stick* (1932) is discussed briefly, Egoff does not include John Buchan's Canadian didactic *Lake of Gold* or *The Long Traverse* (1941), a "time-travel to learn history" set along Québec's Manitou River, written while the author was Governor-General.

Boston/Masefield/Nesbit "ordinary child encounters fantastic in real world" and L.M. Boston's and Kipling's use of fantasy to bring a landscape to life by peopling it with stories. Gwyneth Evans writes of Clark's vivid use of the landscape of the British Columbia interior and observes that through it her books take on "an earthly realism which fortifies the fantasy".[18] "Clark's books are flawed," Evans concludes, "but they contain an originality of vision which is derived not from bookishness but from a deeply tolerant humanity and a loving and close association with the natural environment. Perhaps these qualities will in time help to establish a new, Canadian tradition in fantasy".[19]

The next Canadian fantasist to be discussed in *Worlds Within* is Ruth Nichols. Her works do not stand up well to a demanding reading—her reach exceeded her grasp. However, she made an effort to write serious fantasy, that is, fantasy that takes itself seriously, as opposed to fantasy lacking in humour or whimsy— though Nichols' works are that as well. In many ways Nichols' work is very much in keeping with seventies adult fantasy, and the weaknesses of her stories are those found in much American adult fantasy of the era, a time when writers often imitated the surface of Tolkien and Lewis (badly), and missed entirely the depth.

Nichols' *A Walk Out of the World* (1969) is the story of Tobit and Judith, who walk into another world, where they are proclaimed descendants of past kings. They are immediately involved in a conflict against an ancient, evil usurper and meet various characters, none of whom stand out as having any personality at all, let alone any complex personality. This is a book showing rather stiffly the influence of Tolkien and Lewis, an awed mimicry, half-digested, in creating situations and societies. *A Walk Out of the World* is particularly weak towards the end, when the villain gazes into the innocent child's eyes, sees himself as he truly is, and because of that, commits suicide. After this convenient resolution, an entire war, in which the good side (and there is a good side and a bad side, with nothing to distinguish them but the labels) takes over the kingdom, is dealt with in a paragraph, and

---

[18] Evans, "'Nothing Odd *Ever* Happens Here': Landscape in Canadian Fantasy", *Canadian Children's Literature* No. 15/16, 1980, p. 28.
[19] *ibid.*, p. 28.

Tobit and Judith are sent home, with no real explanation of why they ended up "out of the world" in the first place. All the events of the plot read like a mechanical expansion of an outline. The story lacks the emotional range that would help to bring the characters, their situation, and their world to life. There is no light to balance the dark, no humour, no everyday life in the other world; neither is there any joy, or any attempt to convey the tragedy of civil war. It is bleak, but rather than tragic, it is dull.

Another Nichols book for young adults received the CLA Book of the Year for Children Award for 1973. *The Marrow of the World* (1972) uses a similar framework to Nichols' previous novel. This tells the story of Philip and his cousin Linda, who turns out to be from another world. The two are pulled into that world, where Linda's cruel half-sister, the witch Ygerna, sends her on a mission to find the "marrow of the world", a magical substance which she plans to mix with Linda's blood to increase her own life. All witches, we are told, are evil, pure and simple, and Linda as a half-witch is potentially evil. In the end Linda is said to be giving in to her evil witch side and Philip is helped by the witch-killing king to rescue her. Her ability to cry reveals that she is not actually a witch, and Linda and Philip return to their own world.

Both these books seem on the edge of the "teen problem novel", in that the main characters' unhappiness in their lives is their dominant characteristic, one that is, however, never resolved or even faced up to in the course of the story. It seems merely adopted as a method of outlining a character, something assigned, like hair colour. The characters never grow or demonstrate any change for better or worse. The prose is rather dry and stiff, while the people and worlds never take on life, always seeming made-up. No personality emerges for Nichols' characters beyond their status, established as a label rather than by their actions in the story, as good or evil. *A Walk Out of the World* and *The Marrow of the World* are very dully solemn books, with no spark of humour or glint of light or joy to show why life is worth struggling for. The secondary worlds are likewise very flat; they do not offer the depth and rich detail that convince a reader of their reality, their truth, so essential to good fantasy. No effort is made to show them as living, breathing worlds where real people go about their daily lives, working, suffering, hoping, living, and dying. To adopt Evans' term, Nichols' worlds are created out of "bookishness"; the landscape and societies are generic, with no living detail to wake them into originality and a reality in which readers can immerse themselves.

During the span of time in which Clark and Nichols were writing, early works by a number of giants of the genre were published in Britain and the United States; many of these were destined to become classics. Alan Garner wrote *The Weirdstone of Brisingamen* (1960) and *The Moon of Gomrath* (1963), stories flavoured by Tolkien's world of ancient myth and legend and characters on the scale of heroic epic. In these first two novels by Garner, contemporary children stumble into an ancient and ongoing struggle against forces of darkness. Once enmeshed in that conflict, in which modern humans have no place, they cannot emerge unchanged. Around the same time, Joan Aiken published *The Wolves of Willoughby Chase* (1962), which began the *Wolves Chronicles* of political conspiracy and the supernatural set in an alternate nineteenth-century England; these continued until the posthumous publication of *The Witch of Clatteringshaws* (2005). William Mayne's *A Grass Rope* (1957) takes as its central theme the search for a unicorn in the Yorkshire Dales; like all his books, the psychological complexity of the characters becomes a large part of the environment of the story. His *Earthfasts* (1966) is a time-travel novel, but the traveller comes forward to the present, and his story is not the central focus of the book, which is about ancient, remorseless magics let loose in a small British town, while *It* (1977) again puts a modern protagonist in contact with ancient and dangerous powers, from which she does not free herself without cost and growth. Diana Wynne Jones, whose complex, vividly-realized stories of alternate worlds or matter-of-fact insertion of magic into real world situations in the tradition of Nesbit, as well as her unfailing mastery of comedy and ability to present the realistically strange and potentially tragic in family relationships, continues to gain readers in a new generation. She published her first children's book, *Wilkins' Tooth*, in 1973. *Charmed Life,* the first of Jones' classic (and continuing) Chrestomanci series, using the idea of multiple related worlds (an element which she has made her own and explored in many different ways over her career), came out in 1977. *Cart and Cwidder*, the first of her *Dalemark Quartet* of secondary world fantasies in which young heroes play significant roles in the history of their war-torn land, appeared in 1975, and in 1981, *Time of the Ghost*, a young adult time-travel story in which a disembodied ghost tries to determine who she is, what happened in her childhood that led to her death being demanded by an ancient goddess, and how she can save herself. In all of Jones' books, the heroes are forced to confront truths about themselves in the course of overcoming their external difficulties and enemies; even the very young mature and grow in the course of their adventures.

In the United States, Madeleine L'Engle's *A Wrinkle in Time* began her series about the Murry family and their involvement in the ongoing fight against the powers of hatred and destruction, in 1962. In 1964, Lloyd Alexander's *The Book of Three* launched *The Chronicles of Prydain*, secondary world fantasy drawing on the Welsh matter of the *Mabinogion* in the creation of its world; the hero of the series grows from idealistic boy to thoughtful maturity by the Newbery Medal-winning fifth book *The High King* (1968), becoming king because his experiences have made him worthy of the role, the person the kingdom needs to lead it into a new age. Australia's Patricia Wrightson began her young adult trilogy *The Book of Wirrun*, built on the supernatural of the Australian landscape, with *The Ice Is Coming* (1977), a story which sees the hero ultimately sacrifice his life as a human while trying to protect others. Ursula K. LeGuin attempted secondary world fantasy in her first *Earthsea* book, *A Wizard of Earthsea*, in 1968; her world in that first Earthsea book was thin in conception and somewhat derivative, sometimes seeming founded more on a superficial reading of other writers than on any deep incorporation of ideas into her own imagination. Her exploration of feminist issues led her to continually rethink and deepen that world and its societies, attempting to justify and rationalize her earlier descriptions in light of her own changing thematic concerns and evolving style; the final books in the series, *Tales From Earthsea* and *The Other Wind*, came out in 2001. However, *A Wizard of Earthsea* was a new departure in American fantasy at the time, and is still a classic of the adult genre, although originally regarded as juvenile literature, and the second book in the series, *The Tombs of Atuan*

(1971), which was a Newbery Honor book, successfully portrayed a unique culture and an evolving and complex hero, Tenar, the avatar who is driven to question her religion and her society by the consequences of her own actions. Many other excellent authors of fantasy for children and teens were writing in the sixties, seventies, and early eighties in Great Britain and, although they were fewer in number, in the United States: Eva Ibbotson, John Bellairs, Peter Dickinson, Penelope Lively...to name but a few.

Meanwhile, in Canada, the next author to warrant discussion in Egoff's *Worlds Within* was Janet Lunn. *Double Spell* (1968; *Twin Spell*, 1969 US) is about time-travel that brings children into contact with their own family history. In it, twins Jane and Elizabeth are caught up in events in the past, partly through the medium of an antique doll and partly through a ghost's anger, experiencing episodes in the lives of Anne and Melissa. Anne died in a fire started by her hated cousin Hestor, and the ghost of Hestor haunts the house, tormenting the modern twins, who finally free the ghost and themselves by convincing Hestor that Anne's death was not her fault. (This, despite all the evidence in the story that shows Hestor's fire did cause the girl's death.) The dual agency of the doll and the ghost seems redundant; neither takes primacy as the actual cause of the time-travel; one does not attract the attention of the other, for instance, and the complexity which two links to the past could bring, if each were given its own function, is lacking. The modern twins, by the end, have learnt some family history and brought some modern pop psychology to the ghost; in their own lives, they have merely restored the *status quo* by ending the ghostly disruption, without anything other than a little genealogical knowledge as a result.

Lunn's more famous time-travel story is *The Root Cellar* (1981) (CLA Book of the Year for Children 1982), a "time-travel to learn history", in which Rose Larkin goes back to the eighteen-sixties and the American Civil War by way of an old root-cellar. She makes friends, experiences the life and anxieties of the time, and learns about the people who lived in the house. At the end, there is a very incongruous crossing over of the past into the present, as the people of the past cook a Christmas dinner for those of the present, after Rose's own efforts in the kitchen turn into a disaster. Even in this type of fantasy, more historical fiction in its intent, Canadian writers seemed unsure of themselves, faltering in their ability to keep a story internally consistent. If the magic is, as seems to be the case through most of the book, something limited to Rose and the root-cellar, summoned by powerful emotions and great psychological need, then this abrupt large-scale meeting of worlds for the purpose of salvaging a burnt dinner is illogical and trivializing. Compared with time-travel classics like Alison Uttley's *A Traveller in Time* (1939), *Tom's Midnight Garden* (1958) by Philippa Pearce, or Penelope Farmer's *Charlotte Sometimes* (1969), or books with a time-travel element such as *Earthfasts* (1966) and *Time of the Ghost* (1981), an obvious lack of confidence in the magic of the story, a failure to understand and to trust the aesthetics of fantasy literature, is displayed by this altering of the rules the story has established, this inconsistency in how things work. The magic is reduced to a gimmick at the end, so that the entire experience appears contrived simply as a means of having Rose learn to settle in and live contentedly with her unfamiliar relatives—window-dressing to lure readers into a story intended to illustrate an historical period, or to show Rose becoming a good girl, happy with her new guardians.

Shadow in Hawthorn Bay (1986) (CLA Book of the Year for Children 1988) is perhaps Lunn's most celebrated fantasy. It combines historical fiction and fantasy, being a story about a Scottish girl, Maire, who has second sight. She emigrates to Canada, believing herself summoned by her cousin Duncan, but when she arrives at the new settlement in Upper Canada she discovers Duncan has drowned. His ghost tries to entice her to join him. Most of the story shows how she makes a place for herself in this new community and discovers that she is stronger, more self-sufficient, and not as dependent emotionally on Duncan as she thought. Maire comes to see Upper Canada as a new land free from the Scottish supernatural, a place empty of such things. Its lack of the fantastic is, for her, a liberation.

This is often how the Canadian landscape seems in fantasy set in the real world, historical or contemporary. Despite Catherine Anthony Clark's peopling of the landscape with a mythological spirit world based on native elements, Canadian authors rarely seem to feel a life in the land the way British writers can. Even though Lunn's Maire in this story becomes friends with a native woman, Owena, she never encounters any native supernatural beliefs. In Canada in the seventies and eighties, it seems as if authors could feel or imagine no ancient legends lurking in hill and water that might become the background to a fantasy. Again, this contrasts with the Australian Patricia Wrightson's use of the aboriginal supernatural in her fantasies.

Although Egoff discusses Cora Taylor's *Julie* (1985) (CLA Book of the Year for Children 1986), it contains little fantasy beyond the existence of a psychic and ultimately telekinetic child whose abilities are not the driving force in the story; again, the book primarily functions as a family drama. The fantasy element in this is so slight that if one asks the question, would this, if it were an adult book, be sold as fantasy, the answer would have to be no. Family dramas, romances, mysteries, thrillers, with such a soupçon of the paranormal are the stuff of novels published as "mainstream" rather than fantasy reading.

The final Canadian author to be included in *Worlds Within* is Kit Pearson. Her *A Handful of Time* (1987) (CLA Book of the Year for Children 1987) is another time-travel story, like *The Root Cellar* and *Double Spell*, in which a girl enters her family history, in this case by means of a watch. The protagonist emerges from her experience with a better understanding of her mother and grandmother. The book is not about time-travel or the experience of suddenly being immersed in the past, but about family problems.

Looking beyond Canada, one sees that not all time-travel stories for young people need be about learning history or coming to appreciate family in a new light. The various children in Nesbit's *House of Arden* (1908), *Harding's Luck* (1909), and *The Story of the Amulet* (1906) all have adventures engaging in their own right, regardless of what history a young reader may or may not learn through them, or what the young heroes may learn about their ancestors. Such learning happens as part of the story; it never appears to be the reason for the story to exist. More recent British time-travel classics such as those by Uttley, Pearce, Farmer, Mayne and Jones, are all stories having nothing to do with learning about another time or being educated in family history. Their themes are many and varied, but they are all books that exist to tell a story about a particular character in a particular situation, not as illustrations of a history lesson, even though in some cases a great deal of history may be learnt and understood through reading them.

Humphrey Carpenter and Mari Prichard, in *The Oxford Companion to Children's Literature* (1984) include no Canadian authors in the entry on fantasy,[20] although authors from Australia, Scandinavia, and Germany are mentioned, as well as, of course, significant British and American authors. Even in the entry "Canada",[21] they find little English Canadian fantasy worth mentioning; Clark, Nichols, and Lunn are the only authors discussed. Of these, only Clark and Nichols rate separate entries of their own; both are two to three sentences in length, giving the briefest description of that author's work and no evaluation.

While Egoff and Saltman's discussion of Canadian fantasy of the eighties finds little secondary world fantasy to discuss, such fantasy continued to be a prominent facet of juvenile literature in Britain, and became increasingly so in the United States. Robin McKinley's *The Blue Sword* (1982) was a Newbery Honor book, while *The Hero and the Crown* (1984) won the Newbery Medal; both are secondary world fantasies about young women who claim an unexpected place for themselves as warriors and save the Kingdom of Damar. Brian Jacques began his perennially popular series of heroic animal fantasies with *Redwall* (1986); a series which has continued successfully for twenty years, with new books adding characters and new elements to the world and its history. Tamora Pierce started her career with *Alanna: The First Adventure* (1983), another secondary world series in which the heroic roles are taken by young women. The greats of seventies juvenile fantasy continued to write; Alexander's *Westmark* trilogy (1981-1984) and Jones' *Howl's Moving Castle* (1986) were products of this decade. The dearth of fantasy in Canada was not part of any larger trend in English-language children's literature.

In the marketplace, fantasy has been undervalued in Canada. The remark by the Woozles bookstore representative that prior to 1997 fantasy did not sell does not take account of the fact that

---

[20] Carpenter & Prichard, *Oxford Companion to Children's Literature*, pp. 181-182.

[21] *ibid.*, pp. 94-95.

prior to 1997, Canadian readers looking for children's fantasy in a children's bookstore or the children's section of a general book retailer usually had to resort to special orders, since part of the reason the bookstores sold none was that they did not stock it, or, when they did, they put books such as *Redwall* and *The Golden Compass*, the North American edition of Philip Pullman's Carnegie Medal-winning *His Dark Materials: Northern Lights* (1995), in the adult fantasy section.

That so few examples of Canadian children's fantasy literature can be found for inclusion in surveys and studies such as those of Carpenter and Prichard or Saltman and Egoff is suggestive of the poor quality of Canadian fantasy taken as a whole over much of the twentieth century. It is clear that not since the days of Palmer Cox's *Brownies* (written and published in the United States) has Canadian children's fantasy had any significant impact on the genre at the international level. This may be due in part to the lingering, in the Canadian juvenile literary world, of an early-Victorian, one might even say Calvinistic, suspicion of the fantastic. Any foray into unreality had to be justified by obvious moral worth or its equivalent: some didactic and often narcissistically nationalistic function or "problem book" theme. Even by critics such as Saltman and Egoff, stories with "simple", easily identifiable themes and plots are praised. Those with a complex and novel background (historical, political, geographical or cosmological), any grey areas between "good" and "evil" (such as those often found in political, national, and religious conflicts in the real world), or moral lessons or themes not easily distilled into a single sentence, are criticized for the very literary attributes which can make a book thought-provoking and capable of sustaining repeating readings.

A more recent example of a related attitude may be found in a *CM Magazine* review of the 2005 reissue of J. Fitzgerald McCurdy's *The Serpent's Egg*, which observes that the book "offers little that is new or different in the world of children's fantasy", comments on the "one-dimensional" characters and calls the story "quite predictable...the basic Good vs. Evil fantasy adventure". Yet despite these criticisms, this review praises the book, saying it "will appeal to young fans of 'Harry Potter' or 'The Lord of the Rings'....it will keep an avid fantasy reader happy...".[22] Fantasy, according to this attitude, does not need to be good literature; it need only present certain stereotypes and follow a prescribed simple pattern to appeal to the same readers who enjoy what has been declared the greatest novel of the twentieth century, *The Lord of the Rings*.[23] Similarly, a review of Terry Griggs' *The Silver Door* in the same journal remarks on parts of the book that "don't seem to add anything to the story" but concludes this is not a flaw because "the beauty of fantasy lies in the fact that things don't have to make sense as long as they titillate the imagination".[24] Something in a work of fiction that stimulates the imagination might possibly be admitted to actually be adding something to the story, but the statement that fantasy is a genre where "things don't have to make sense" is another example of the belief that labelling a work "fantasy" excuses poor craftsmanship, poor art.

Fantasy readers, this attitude holds, have no discrimination, no ability to judge between good prose and bad, good storytelling and the mediocre, between depth and derivation. One could say this of nearly all juvenile readers before they have read broadly or in quantity, no matter what their tastes in books. As in most matters, experience is the foundation of judgement. However, that offers no excuse for presenting them with poorly written, slipshod literature, no excuse for saying that quality does not matter because children cannot tell the difference. And suggesting that because a work is fantasy, literary standards should be lower, belittles the work of the many fantasy authors who take their art seriously, and displays a condescending attitude to those numerous readers who take fantasy literature seriously. A fantasy with a stereotypical, simplistic plot and two dimensional characters, with episodes that add nothing to the story and its world, inserted for novelty or to stretch out a thin plot without regard for internal co-

---

[22] Ann Ketcheson. *CM Magazine* Volume XII, Number 18, May 12, 2006. http://www.umanitoba.ca/outreach/cm/vol12/no18/theserpentsdegg.htm

[23] In a poll conducted by the BBC programme *Book Choice* and the chain bookseller Waterstone's, and again by the *Daily Telegraph* newspaper. Cited in T.A. Shippey. *J.R.R. Tolkien: Author of the Century*. London: HarperCollins, 2000. xx-xxi.

[24] Kristin Butcher. *CM Magazine* Volume X, Number 20, June 4, 2004. http://www.umanitoba.ca/outreach/cm/vol10/no20/thesilverdoor.html

herency or integrity, is more likely to find wide and enduring appeal among those who are *not* serious fantasy readers, child or adult, and who are not "fans" of *The Lord of the Rings*, because it does not demand much effort from its readers. Because such fantasy is superficial, no imaginative effort is required to enter the world and the mind of the characters and accept that their world is different, their experiences different, their ways of looking of the world unfamiliar and shaped by circumstances other than the reader's own; no deep attention is needed to experience the work in its fullness. A school story with flat, stereotyped characters and disjointed events would not be praised and recommended because it is a school story and thus expected to be of poor literary quality. Such a work would not be compared to great school stories as if the setting were all that was required to make them equals in quality of literary experience for the reader. Fantasy is not an excuse for poor writing.

Because fantasy asks readers, while reading, to accept as true and real within the context of the story things that the rational mind knows cannot be possible, it demands good writing; fantasy cannot work without attention to internal consistency, without adherence to the rules of reality set within the story. It absolutely must make sense. Even the apparently chaotic merging of characters and settings into one another in Lewis Carroll's *Alice's Adventures in Wonderland* and *Through the Looking-Glass* makes sense and adheres to the rules Carroll has established for his dream world; this very chaos and fluidity defines the world in which Alice has found herself. Coleridge, writing of an intention to use the supernatural in a narrative poem, said that it would require "a semblance of truth sufficient to procure for these shadows of imagination that willing suspension of disbelief for the moment, which constitutes poetic faith".[25] Lewis, in *An Experiment in Criticism*, uses the term "realism of presentation" and defines it as "the art of bringing something close to us, making it palpable and vivid, by sharply observed or sharply imagined detail".[26] He proceeds to offer several examples of this, taken from sources ranging from *Beowulf* and Layamon's *Brut* to Shakespeare and

---

[25] *Biographia Literaria*, p. 442.
[26] *An Experiment in Criticism*, p. 57.

Wordsworth, and notes that the examples he has chosen, though he did not, he claims, choose them for that purpose, are all found in "stories which are not themselves at all 'realistic' in the sense of being probable or even possible."[27] He contrasts this with "realism of content", which is found when the story is "probable or 'true to life'".[28] Elsewhere, Lewis remarks that, "Multiplication of enchantments is no proof that the writer is himself enchanted; it rather suggest that they are to him mere stage properties."[29] He continues with the observation that "homely details" are demanded by the "devoutly romantic" reader of fairy-tales, "because their absence hinders the serious suspension of disbelief which he wishes to make."[30] A weak fantasy is one in which the fantasy, rather than being given reality by attention to a semblance of truth or reality of presentation, is itself the detail, the decoration scattered over the surface of a thin tale. Tolkien, in "On Fairy-Stories", says of "a successful 'sub-creator'" that such a story-teller "makes a Secondary World which your mind can enter. Inside it, what he relates is 'true': it accords with the laws of that world. You therefore believe it, while you are, as it were, inside".[31] This is what he termed "literary belief". In a poor fantasy, there is no accordance with the laws of the world of the story, no internal consistency. "Not making sense" is as much a flaw in a fantasy story as in any other, but only in fantasy is the type of fiction itself made an excuse or even justification for a lack of internal consistency, as though fantasy is some inadequate and feeble member of the literary family for whom allowances must be made.

Fantasy exists in part to do what other species of literature cannot do to the same degree, to hold a transforming mirror to reality. It reflects or brings into prominence what is ignored; throws light into dark corners; drags shadows out into view and gives fears a shape to be recognized and confronted; asks the "what if" questions. It shows the power of the individual to take a stand, and reminds that heroes are heroes for the choices they

---

[27] *ibid.* p. 58.
[28] *ibid.* p. 59.
[29] C.S. Lewis, "The *Morte Darthur*", in *Studies in Medieval and Renaissance Literature*, p.107.
[30] *ibid.*
[31] *The Monsters and the Critics and Other Essays* p. 132.

make and the actions they take, even when their cause seems hopeless—all in a reality that is not *quite* that of the audience. *Gilgamesh, The Iliad,* and *Beowulf,* "East of the Sun, West of the Moon" and "The Seven Ravens", are all something quite different from the fables of Aesop or the pre-*Alice* children's novels of the nineteenth century. It is that quality of otherness, of grand possibilities both good and terrible, of mystery in the older sense of the word, which is rendered impossible when the fantasy in a story is used merely as an excuse not to bother considering the laws of reality, as a shortcut to historical fiction, or to dress up a lesson. Unfortunately, the latter uses have from the start been the fate of fantasy in most Canadian writing for children.

Has the current upsurge of interest in juvenile fantasy resulted, at the opening of the twenty-first century (the years between 2000 and 2004), in any movement away from earlier trends in the genre in this country? That is, has Canadian children's fantasy moved beyond the need to demonstrate obvious didactic value by imparting heavily underscored moral or historical lessons? Has fantasy in Canadian children's literature become more than mere window-dressing? By window-dressing is meant the use of fantasy elements in a shallow or superficial way, fantasy that is not fully integrated to the story or inherent to it, but which appears to be added as either an excuse for unreality, or a bit of eye-catching novelty. Sometimes such a use of fantasy is the result of an author who has scavenged some ideas from a few popular books or television shows and who lacks any familiarity with or understanding of the traditions of fantasy. In many cases, though, the window-dressing of fantasy is intended as the spoonful of sugar to sweeten the lesson, as in the historical fiction novel disguised as time-travel fantasy, in which a modern child is whisked back to witness the past and interpret it for the reader, usually by some magical device which plays little role in actually shaping the story. (This device generally lacks even any magic in its nature to render it other than an obvious plot convenience, hastily abandoned once the real story begins; there is no developed context into which the means of time-travel fits, no consistency in the rules of the world.) The lesson the reader is meant to take away from such dressed-up stories, whether they be time-travel or other varieties of fantasy, is explicit, all but pointed out and underlined. In good fantasy, by contrast, what lessons there are, are implicit: they are present, and they have more impact, *because* they are contained within an engrossing story, but they are not the first impression nor the dominant element in the tale.

This self-consciously didactic and moralizing bent is at least partially to blame for the past weakness of the genre in Canada; where fantasy is merely a tool or a decoration, there is no impetus to make it more than superficial. If Canadian fantasy writing published for children in the period 2000 to 2004 is moving beyond "window-dressing", the maturing of the genre in Canada may result in the production of works able to be classed with the best coming out of Britain and the United States. If, in twenty years, there is another study such as *Worlds Within* (or another *Quests and Kingdoms*) will there be more than six (or four)[32] Canadian authors included?

---

[32] The four in *Quests and Kingdoms: A Grown-Up's Guide to Children's Fantasy Literature*, are Charles de Lint, Dave Duncan, O.R. Melling, and Kenneth Oppel.

II
TIME-TRAVEL

TIME-TRAVEL IS FOUND IN BOTH fantasy and science fiction. In science fiction, the act of travelling through time is given a quasi-scientific explanation based on speculations about the nature of the universe, whereas in fantasy it is accomplished by magic of some sort. The magic may be inherent in an object, a creature, or person, or caused by some affinity between people of different times, or it may lie in a particular place which acts as a bridge between times. Often the only fantastic element in a time-travel fantasy is the travel through time, but in the great stories, the time-travel does not function solely as a means of setting a modern child protagonist in place to witness the past. The experiences of the characters as they enter another time are of interest in their own right. A great deal about the past may be revealed, or the protagonist may be followed through a period of significant growth, but the story is often also *about* travelling in time. The travel is not a convenience, but something of significance that affects those experiencing it. The purpose of the heroes is not to see the past, but is some other adventure for which the past acts as a setting, often strange, intriguing, and presenting as many difficulties as a journey to a foreign land. In Nesbit's *The Story of the Amulet* (1906), the children are in search of the other half of a magic amulet, in order to obtain their heart's desire. In *The House of Arden* (1908), the quest is for a treasure. In Uttley's *A Traveller in Time* (1939), a girl drifts into the past of a house at the time of a plot to rescue Mary Queen of Scots from imprisonment; she finds she has a place in both times, and the *story* is about how suspicion that she is an agent of Elizabeth almost brings about tragedy, as well as the quiet sorrow of the doomed love between her and a young man in the past. Never does the purpose of the story seem to be to illustrate "the failure of the Babbington plot" (the central historical event of the book). In Pearce's *Tom's Midnight Garden* (1958), loneliness draws Tom and Hetty together across time, and any illustration of life two generations before Tom's day is a result of the story; it occurs while the story about Tom and Hetty unfolds. There is no self-conscious instruction.

A more recent example of an excellent time-travel story is found in Rumiko Takahashi's 1997 manga *Inuyasha*, in which Kagome, a Japanese girl of the late twentieth century, is pulled five hundred years into the past through an ancient well in her family's shrine. She becomes involved in a quest to keep the shards of a shattered jewel of great power from falling into the hands of a nihilistic demon. Her connection to the past is an intrinsic part of the story; she is the reincarnation of a Shinto priestess, who was murdered and cremated with the jewel, the object which enabled Kagome to pass through the well. The story is about her growth as a hero as she creates a place for herself among the enemies of the demon Naruko and struggles to reconcile the two times to which she has come to belong, about the changes she brings to the lives of her new comrades, and, to a lesser degree, about the influence of past and future on one another through Kagome's travels back and forth. Again, the time-travel is a fundamental part of the story, not a tool to facilitate some end external to the tale. Another example is Terry Pratchett's *Johnny and the Bomb* (1996), the third in his Johnny Maxwell trilogy set in late twentieth-century England. Johnny (around whom reality becomes unnervingly fluid) worries about a stray German bomb that hit his town in 1941 and becomes entangled with bag-lady Mrs Tachyon's mysteriously squishy black bags of time. The story is about movements between alternate pasts and futures and their effects on people's lives, not "Johnny learns about the Blitz".

On the other hand, in Kipling's *Puck of Pook's Hill* (1906) and *Rewards and Fairies* (1910), magic brings two children and a series of people from the past together. The children do not travel to the past, but instead meet people of other times to learn their stories. However, the magic permitting this is not a device superimposed on the story, ignored once its function is fulfilled. Instead, it is an integral part of the plot of the framing narrative which surrounds each story. The children accidentally summon Puck, who remains their friend, telling them his own stories and introducing them to his friends from across time because he believes they need to "take seizin" of the land their father owns, to truly come to feel a part of its long history themselves. The purpose of the books is to evoke the romance of British history, particularly of that corner of Sussex in which Kipling was living, but that purpose does not overshadow the stories. The tales told by Puck, Parnesius, Sir Richard and the others they meet run from the Stone Age to the dissolution of the monasteries and beyond, but each holds its own interest, independent of the framing narrative, and could stand on its own: a story of adventure, tragedy, great achievement, or some turning point in the narrator's life. The frame story likewise holds its own interest, as Dan and Una discover a little more about Puck and his connections to the characters they meet and the landscape about them.

Like Kipling's, Canadian time-travel stories have sometimes attempted, as in Buchan's *Lake of Gold* (1941), to illustrate history; more often, as in Lunn's *The Root Cellar* (1968) and *Double Spell* (1981), and Pearson's *A Handful of Time* (1987), they portray characters for whom time-travel is a means to encounter family history. Inevitably, the time-travel has been a device serving these ends. It has not soared into story itself, as it does even in the historical vignettes of *Puck of Pook's Hill*.

Ghost Voyages II: The Matthew (J)[1]

Cora Taylor's first novel was *Julie* (see page 14). Among her other early books was *The Doll* (1987), a time-travel in which a doll takes the heroine into the past while she recovers from illness; more recently, she has written straight historical fiction (the *Angelique* books for Penguin's *Our Canadian Girl* series) and some engaging young adult secondary world fantasies (see page 109).

Taylor's *Ghost Voyages II: The Matthew* (2002) is a sequel to her *Ghost Voyages* (1992), another time-travel. Ten-year-old Jeremy uses the magic of his grandfather's collection of ship stamps to travel in time, in order to escape problems at home following his parents' divorce. In this second book, his stress is caused by his father's attempt to get custody of him, which is sparked by his

---

[1] *J* (juvenile or children approximately 8-13) and *YA* ("young adult" or teens approximately 12+) are indicated merely as the most likely readership.

impoverished mother's request for larger support payments. Jeremy decides he needs a bit of time-travel to help him with his misery, gets out the stamp album and magnifying glass, and picks his destination. He chooses the maiden voyage of the *Bluenose II*. Not only is the method of time-travel overly simple and convenient, but there seems little risk involved. Jeremy views a stamp through the magnifying glass and is immediately present in the past as a ghost, unable to be seen or heard or to affect events. Moreover, as if drowsing, he remains remotely aware of things going on around him in his own time. After dropping in on the *Bluenose II* he travels to Cabot's ship the *Matthew* in 1497. Here a sailor immediately accuses another of having had too much rum, over a century before that liquor existed. In a time-travel book, details of the past should be as accurate as historical knowledge and archaeology allow, if the historical aspect of the story is to have any value.

On the *Matthew*, Jeremy meets another ghostly time-traveller, Harv, who provides the means for Jeremy to solve his problems in the present. Harv is his grandfather, so Jeremy finds out which stamps will be valuable in his own time, asks Harv to collect them and place them in the album, and then sells them to a stamp dealer, from whom he also gets a job.

Although Taylor writes well, the story is overly simplistic. The time-travel is too obviously a convenience, provided merely as stress-relief for Jeremy. It does little even to illustrate the past he visits, and despite his fears during a storm, neither he nor Harv ever encounter any real difficulties in the past or face any decision requiring choice and action. They are passive observers, but little is offered for them to observe that will even serve a "time-travel to learn history" end, let alone force them to take action and grow. The stories Jeremy witnesses, unlike those in Kipling's *Puck of Pook's Hill*, are mere glimpses of moments devoid of any narrative continuity. His journeys to the past offer piecemeal snapshots, not even of the lives of the sailors or the excitement of exploration, but mostly of storms. The magic of the stamps is nothing more than a simple, safe diversion for an anxious child and an equally simple solution to his problems. It is too easy; one is never convinced that the magic has any independent reality beyond its service to Jeremy.

Tunnels of Time (J)

Tunnels of Time (2000) is the first of Mary Harelkin Bishop's time-travel series about the Moose Jaw tunnels, which extend under the city of Moose Jaw and are said to have been used by Chinese immigrants and by bootleggers in the early decades of the twentieth century. When Andrea Talbot bumps her head on a mirror in one of the tunnels, she finds herself in the nineteen-twenties. Mistaken for a boy, she gets work as a runner, carrying messages through the tunnels for bootlegging gangsters to warn of police raids and guiding people through the tunnels for the gangsters. After she, her friend Vance, and Vance's sister Beanie tip off the police to raid the gangsters' base, she reveals the truth about herself to Beanie. Andrea then returns to the present following another bump on the head. There, her embarrassingly eccentric Great-Aunt Bea reveals that she is Beanie and Vance is Andrea's grandfather. Subsequent books in the series, which are Bishop's only published fiction to date, are *Tunnels of Terror* (2001), *Tunnels of Treachery* (2003), and *Tunnels of Tyranny* (2005). These send Andrea and her younger brother Tony into the tunnels of the past to take part in stories involving crime, racism, and the Ku Klux Klan, and to follow the development of Vance's career as a journalist.

Aside from the very weak explanation for the time-travel, the story is well constructed. The historical research is on the whole accurate and is presented in an engaging fashion.[2] The description of the tunnels is particularly vivid. The historical material is well woven into the plot. The adventure is not made subservient to the illustration of this colourful period of Moose Jaw's history; it always seems to be a story about Andrea's adventures, which brings a certain time and place to life, rather than an illustration of a particular historical fact. By the fourth book, though, this balance changes, and the manipulation of the plot to illustrate various aspects and sins of the past becomes more obvious; Andrea's adventures seem more noticeably contrived. Throughout the series,

---

[2] However, a review by Tony Payzant notes that in the second book in the series, flashlights are greeted with astonishment, though they had by then existed for several decades. *CM Magazine* Volume VIII Number 14, March 15, 2002 http://www.umanitoba.ca/outreach/cm/vol8/no14/tunnels.html

the time-travel itself is merely a device to put a modern protagonist into a story set in the nineteen-twenties, in order to explain historical detail to the modern child. As a device, the bump on the head seems a poor excuse, belonging more to *Looney Tunes* than to a novel, and by book four, entering the tunnels with a desire to visit the past seems to be enough to make the time-travel happen. Since they are not stories *about* the experience of time-travel, as are *Tom's Midnight Garden* or *A Traveller in Time*, and take place in a world otherwise lacking magic, unlike Nesbit's various time-travel books, the underlying fantasy premise never convinces us of its reality and remains an obvious mechanical device, a shortcut to making the past "accessible". They are good adventure stories, but their fantasy element is mere window-dressing.

The Mystery of the Medieval Coin (J)

Prior to *The Mystery of the Medieval Coin* (2004), A.D. Fast had written only real-world "problem" novels for teens, dealing with such themes as eating disorders, gangs, and hockey violence. Fast's *The Mystery of the Medieval Coin* is a "time-travel to learn history". Three students travel into the past through the combination of a medieval coin stolen from a teacher's desk and a cave with a mysterious inscription. The teacher, Mr. LeClair, is obsessed with "feudalism"—a word used inappropriately where the manorial system and the legal state of villeinage appear to be meant[3]—and believes the world would be better if peasants still

---

[3] Feudalism is a system of landholding in which the vassal, a free man (less often a woman or a religious community) owes his overlord service, usually military, in return for land. A good explanation for the layman is found in *The National Trust Historical Atlas of Britain: Prehistoric to Medieval Britain*, which states that the origins of feudalism lie in the practice "among the greater lords of entrusting estates to followers in return not for rent, but for specific services, usually military..." (p. 110). Manorialism, the system whereby the land of a manor was worked by a combination of free and unfree tenants, and villeinage, the existence of a large class of unfree villeins or serfs bound to the land of a particular manor, are not the same as feudalism. In the manorial system, serfs or villeins were beholden to their lords "for their land, for their house, even for the tools of their trade. They could not leave the manor without their permission..." (ibid. p. 155), or, as the OED says under "**manorial system**": "a system of social, political, and economic organization practised widely in medieval Europe, in which peasants and free tenants were rendered dependent on their lord for land tenure and the administration of local justice...The manorial system was

knew their place. The students pursue LeClair into the past through the "portal" in the cave and find themselves in the dungeon of a castle in France in 1450, where they discover that Mr. LeClair appears to be King Charles VII. They witness a feast and a joust, discover that medieval moats are full of sewage, and return to their own time. They conclude that LeClair intends to suppress the printing of books by Gutenberg's press (in German Mainz!), thereby preventing social change and the decline of feudalism.

That the alteration of any one element alone could fossilize a society as dynamic as that of fifteenth-century Europe, which was in a constant process of change, internal debate, evolution and outright revolution, and that without Gutenberg no one would *ever, ever* have developed movable type, are not premises that can bear any examination. Such a simplistic presentation of historical processes certainly has no place in a book intended to develop a child's interest in history. The book is weak in other elements as well. There seems little reason for the dual mechanism of coin and cave. Utterly no reason is given for a modern Canadian cave to connect to a medieval French "dungeon", or for the coin and the cave to have any magical connection, as it seems they must. Medieval details are superficially researched at best. Not only is "feudalism" used incorrectly (no minor detail but the villain's primary motivation and thus a central idea in the story), there are other inaccuracies. Despite what children will mislearn from this story, which claims to be representing factual historical detail, the donjon or dungeon of a castle was not some underground cellar, but the keep, a tower that was the primary stronghold and into the fourteenth century often the residential part of the castle. The word's use to mean a place of imprisonment is found in the middle ages, but as an architectural feature, a part of the castle, the dungeon was a strong tower and often the home of the lord, not a sodden cellar full of prisoners.

Lack of historical accuracy is not the novel's only flaw. The plot moves slowly, dragging out minor mysteries without any de-

---

intimately connected with the feudal system, but historians distinguish between the two on the basis that the manorial system did not involve estates held in fief" (Oxford English Dictionary Online, 2007).

velopment. Characters exhibit no development whatsoever. Dialogue is rendered inconsistently, mixing current slang with stiffly formal, unrealistically contraction-free utterances on the part of the children. One child stays up every night for a week, watching his teacher disappear into the cave, but remains bright, alert, and even-tempered throughout the day. The story also ends on an abrupt anticlimax with nothing resolved—neither a natural pause in the story, wrapping up one phase before a continuance in the promised sequel, or a cliffhanger. As a story, *The Mystery of the Medieval Coin* is thin and unsatisfying; as a story meant to capture the imaginations of readers and either inspire an interest in medieval history or teach something about the period, it is ill-executed and merely reinforces the vague and superficial impressions of hackneyed television shows. Its fantasy element, the time-travel magic of cave and coin, is mere window-dressing, a weak device the sole function of which is to take the children into the past, and which has no thematic relation to anything else in the story.

Time and Again (YA)

Another recent book in which two times are bridged by the protagonist is *Time and Again* (2004) by Deb Loughead, whose previous publications were largely humorous stories and poetry for younger children. As is so often the case with time-travel, *Time and Again* teaches a lesson, although not so blatantly as Fast's *The Mystery of the Medieval Coin*. The main character, Kate, is characterized primarily by her jealousy of her sports-star brother; by the end of the book she has reconciled with her parents and realized, through witnessing some of what her teenage great-aunt Kathleen experienced while suffering from tuberculosis in the thirties, that her own problems are much more manageable than those many have faced. Kate spends the summer on her grandparents' farm, upset that the farm is for sale, passing her time in swimming and jogging with the teenage "farmhands" imported from Toronto—perhaps the least likely place in Canada from which to recruit dairymen. Although allegedly a dairy farm in the summer, there is no evidence that anyone actually cuts hay, makes silage, milks the cows, or in fact does any farmwork at all—although on one occasion a "farmhand" does paint a fence.

Kate either sees a ghost or enters visions of the past; these exist as means of showing Kate what her great-aunt's life was like; they also help to solve the mystery of how she actually died. Furthermore, by finding a letter in the family Bible which somehow no-one has ever come across before, Kate discovers a cache of banknotes initially hidden by Kathleen's aunt and moved by Kathleen just before her death. Kate's abduction by one of the "farmhands", who is looking for this treasure himself, and her ghost-aided resistance to and escape from him, provide a dramatic climax to the plot. *Time and Again* is better-crafted and more convincing than *The Mystery of the Medieval Coin*, although its strength lies primarily in its well-rendered portrayal of first love. Both its real-world setting and its fantastic elements are unbelievable, the former because the details that would give the farm reality are not there, and what is there distracts by its implausibility, and the latter because the ghost, and Kate's contact with the past, are emotionless compared to other well-handled, emotion-filled elements of the story. The ghost and Kate's experience of the past through her connection to it do not evoke any sense of wonder or fear on their own part to touch the emotion or imagination, merely leading Kate to resolve mysteries in her family history. The fantasy element functions as an obvious plot device.

ALTHOUGH TIME-TRAVEL REMAINS a common device in Canadian children's literature, it has changed little over the decades. At the turn of the millennium time-travel is still used as quick device for creating an illusion of identification between the youthful reader and the protagonist in an historical fiction. It is also treated as a fast and easy tool to enable a character to explore family history and solve present-day problems—time-travel as therapy. The time-travel is not effected by means of ancient magic, by items with a provenance relevant to the story or creatures capable of transcending time; it has no roots in the past. There is no history of magic to Taylor's stamps, Fast's coin and cave, or Bishop's tunnels, no reason within the story for the single point of magic in an otherwise magicless world. When the time-travel arises from a resonance between past and present acting on a particular character, as with Kate and her great-aunt in *Time and Again*, the focus of the story is not the experience of time-travel and the participation in another life, but a "count your blessings" lesson coupled with the solution of a family mystery. Time-travel remains an obvious device, a quick and easy means of linking past and present, rather than something to be explored in its own right.

III
MAGIC IN THE PRIMARY WORLD

A WIDE RANGE OF BOOKS EXISTS in which magic enters the everyday world, the real or primary world. Stories of this type may be lighthearted, as in nearly all of the fantasy works of E. Nesbit (1902's *Five Children and It*, etc.), and Mary Norton's *The Borrowers* (1952) and its sequels, Penelope Lively's *The Revenge of Samuel Stokes* (1981), or Diana Wynne Jones' *The Ogre Downstairs* (1974), or more serious in what is at stake, as in Jones' *Time of the Ghost* (1981) or *Dogsbody* (1975). The primary world magic may also take the form of ancient opposing forces continuing a long struggle into which modern children, by fate or chance, are drawn, as in Alan Garner's *The Weirdstone of Brisingamen* (1960) and *The Moon of Gomrath* (1963) and Susan Cooper's five-book series *The Dark is Rising* (1965-1977), which began with *Over Sea, Under Stone*; the second book in the sequence, *The Dark is Rising* (1973), was a Newbery Honor book, while book four, *The Grey King* (1975) won the Newbery Medal. In many such stories, the magic consists of traditional supernatural beings or is created on a foundation of traditional beliefs about magic. The heroes encounter creatures from folklore, legend, and myth, or discover that old spells and prophecies, or objects with traditions of enchantment attached to them, are truly magical, capable of bringing them into contact with a world they had thought only imaginary.

It is far more rare for the magic in such a book to be something new, without a foundation in tradition, as are the luminaries, avatars of the stars and planets in *Dogsbody*. Even the tiny people in *The Borrowers* build on familiarity with numerous older traditions of little (often fairy) folk, while the seven powerful siblings in Jones' *Archer's Goon* (1984), who are gangsters and engineers rather than any traditional sort of magic-users, are described by another character as "wizards", which provides a quick frame of reference for young readers, though their behaviour is far from wizardly in any familiar sense. In contrast, Eva Ibbotson's many books, such as *Which Witch?* (1979), *The Secret of Platform 13* (1994), and *Island of the Aunts* (1999), Jill Murphy's *The Worst Witch* (1974), and J.K. Rowling's *Harry Potter and the Philosopher's Stone* (1997) use familiar conventions about witches, ghosts, and other supernatural creatures.

In Canadian fantasy, Cox's nineteenth-century *Brownies* used one Scottish fairy tradition to teach and explore the world. The books of Catherine Anthony Clark in the nineteen-fifties and -sixties brought magic into the primary world in her stories of ordinary children having adventures with traditional and invented aboriginal supernatural beings in the wilderness of British Columbia. Taylor's *Julie* (1985) used the tradition of "second sight"; in the nineteen-eighties and -nineties Welwyn Wilton Katz and Michael Bedard wrote stories of youths encountering dangerous supernatural powers familiar to popular culture—witches, evil forces of hatred and destruction, and in the case of Bedard's Governor-General's Award winning dark fantasy for teens, *Redwork* (1990), alchemy.

Stories of magic encountered by ordinary children in the primary world, particularly when that magic is of a form traditional and familiar to readers from popular culture, as in the books of Ibbotson, Murphy, and Rowling, have great appeal to those who are not dedicated fantasy readers. Because the magic in primary world stories often uses traditional elements, such stories may be more readily picked up by the non-fantasy reader than a secondary world fantasy. An invented world and culture demand greater imaginative involvement on the part of the reader, who must learn about the new world while reading the story. A tale of magic set in the primary world provides a familiar cultural context for the reader. The exotic and unfamiliar enters the known world; it may even be not so unfamiliar: ghosts, fairies, a wish-granting ring...elements such as these may be recognized by the reader, with their history and attributes requiring little explanation as the story unfolds. Other magics and magical beings may be traditional but unfamiliar within the reader's cultural context; such stories are often able to introduce new imaginative worlds and the cultural traditions of other lands to readers who might never pick up a book on folklore or a collection of myths.

The Loki Wolf (J/YA)

The Loki Wolf (2000) is the third in Arthur G. Slade's *Northern Frights* series of dark fantasy for teens. It follows *Draugr* (1997) and *The Haunting of Drang Island* (1998). Based on Icelandic myth and folklore, these feature various combinations of three teen characters, Icelandic-American cousins Angie, Michael, and Sarah, and their Icelandic grandfather from Gimli, Manitoba. In *The Loki Wolf* all three cousins and their grandfather travel to Iceland, where they encounter shapeshifting werewolves, one of whom has an ancient bloodfeud with their family. The teens are thrown upon their own resources and forced to find inner cores of strength and endurance, to survive the dangers and salvage hope and love from tragedy. Angie's final, lonely confrontation with the ancient werewolf Skoll is as heroic, thrilling and moving as a last stand in a saga (although it turns out better for the hero than such battles usually do). All three books in the series are well-written, with convincing and likeable characters. The folkloric element is well-integrated into the modern world, the historical detail is good, and Slade, who writes historical fiction as well as fantasy, seems to have researched his Norse and Icelandic material thoroughly. The *Northern Frights* series is a good example of the use of traditional folkloric elements in a modern setting; it also tells great stories worth more than a single reading.

The Keeper and the Crows (J)

Andrea Spalding is the author or co-author of a number of picture and early chapter books, about half of which are fantasy. Spalding's *The Keeper and the Crows* (2000) is written for beginning novel-readers, using simple language and short words. It tells the story of Misha's visit to the house of Dora, his aunt. She is the guardian of a box containing hope; her duty is to unlock it every morning to release a little hope into the world. However, the spare key, usually guarded by a fish, has been stolen by crows, who want to gain power by acquiring the box. How this will give them power is not explained.

As in many works specifically written to be "beginning chapter books", characterization is flat and there is no growth and development even for the hero. The plot is structured largely on coincidences, culminating in Misha's stumbling upon the crow hoard and the missing key. Although the fantasy element, Misha's quest for the key to the box of hope, is the foundation of the story, the justification for the conflict (what are the crows planning to do with the box of hope anyway?) is so weak that the work fails to function as a believable whole.

An additional problem with this book is the apparently unwitting expropriation of Tolkien's riddle "Alive without breath". In a note at the end, the author claims that the four lines used for Dora's sturgeon-summoning spell are "one of the oldest riddles in the English language".[1] Her error may be due to ignorance or to inadequate research; she does not cite her source for the claim that the poem is ancient. The claim of antiquity is in error. The verse is an original composition by Tolkien (with the word "ever" misquoted by Spalding as "always"). Tolkien wrote the riddle for *The Hobbit* and then, expanded and with a few changes to the wording, included it in *The Lord of the Rings* in the chapter "The Passage of the Marshes";[2] it is this version which is used with its true author unacknowledged in *The Keeper and the Crows*. Tolkien's verse should certainly not have been used without proper acknowledgement and citation; given that it is not included as a *quoted* riddle or poem but in a completely different context which makes it appear to be an integral part of another's work of fiction,

---

[1] Spalding, *The Keeper and the Crows*, p. 122.

[2] Of the sources of the riddles in *The Hobbit*, Shippey writes "Gollum's 'Time' riddle in *The Hobbit* is based on Saturn's 'Old Age' one [in the Old English poem *Solomon and Saturn II*]" (footnote, p. 133 in *The Road to Middle-earth*, 2nd Edn. London: HarperCollins, 1992). The lines in *Solomon and Saturn II* (ll. 297-306) to which Shippey refers might be better described as "loose inspiration" rather than "foundation for" Tolkien's riddle: both are framed as a series of questions, but the questions are not the same. Tolkien himself wrote, "As for the Riddles: they are 'all my own work' except for 'Thirty White Horses' which is traditional, and 'No-legs'. The remainder, though their style and method is that of old literary...riddles, have *no models* as far as I am aware, save only the egg-riddle..." (p. 123, letter 110, in Carpenter, *The Letters of J.R.R. Tolkien,* Boston: Houghton Mifflin, 1981). The fish riddle "Alive without breath" is nowhere attributed to any previous source and is not found among the corpus of Old English riddles. (Even had it been Tolkien's translation of an Old English original, any version in rhymed Modern English by Tolkien would have been his own, and like any other translation, subject to copyright and not something to be quoted without proper credit to the author/translator and source being given.)

it is doubtful that it should have been included at all. The publisher has said that the error of attribution will be corrected in any future editions of *The Keeper and the Crows* (pers. corr.).

The Summer of Magic Quartet (J)

The White Horse Talisman (2001) is the first of a four-book series by Andrea Spalding. The heroes of the story are four children, Canadians Adam and Chantal, and their British cousins Holly and Owen. Adam and Chantal have been sent to their relatives while their parents struggle with the failure of their marriage. In present-day England, they encounter ancient magic. To save the Wise Ones, the children must find magical items hidden from the Dark One. Chantal is declared a Magic Child by the Uffington White Horse (a stylized figure carved into the chalk of Oxfordshire, probably in the late Iron Age). Adam's resentment of Chantal, who is always the centre of attention, and his anger at his parents leaves him vulnerable to being used by the Dragon, an enemy of the Wise Ones.

Alan Garner and Susan Cooper are among the best writers of fantasy in which children encounter old magic with its roots deep in English landscape and folklore. *The White Horse Talisman* falls short of that level of greatness, lacking the depth and complexity needed to give it reality. The Wise Ones leave nothing for the children to achieve on their own in the course of the quest; the protagonists' every step is guided by the spirits. Chantal is told through her dreams where the missing half of the talisman should be; discovering it is simply a matter of asking a local historian where to find the place. Potential for failure comes only in Adam's struggle with himself and the Dragon's temptation.

Although characterization and plot are simplistic, the tension between Adam and Chantal is very realistic and credible. The effect on both siblings of the stress of their parents' failing marriage is well handled.

The story contains several dream-journeys into the past on Chantal's part, which introduce errors of historical detail, such as anachronistic Iron Age British stirrups and ninth-century Anglo-Saxon inns. A more serious fault in historical presentation is the suggestion in the prologue that the name England arises from "Angel Land", these "Angels" being, by their place in the chronology of events, a Celtic or pre-Celtic people. In a work intended to be rooted in real history and archaeology, this seems an unnecessary and misleading piece of invention, particularly since many children form their first understanding of the vast sweep of the past from reading fiction. Few children will be aware that the Angles, about whom Pope Gregory the Great made his celebrated angel pun, were a later people who displaced the Celts, and most may end up with a very confused idea of the succession of peoples in Britain. In contrast to this bit of unannotated historical misdirection, Spalding's afterword notes where she has deviated from reality in describing the scouring of the hill-figures. This conscientiousness only makes the failure to distinguish historical fact from invention in the matter of her Angels more inexplicable.

Dance of the Stones (2003) continues the story, as the birdwoman Ava seeks Owen's aid in recovering a circlet buried at Avebury and an ancient oak tree needs Holly's help to save it from being felled. More detail about the Wise Ones' enemy, now called "the Evil One", is given, although that detail is fairly superficial: the Evil One is returning as a dark cloud covering the galaxy, with little motivation or past. This is very reminiscent of the Black Thing, the shadow that blots out the stars as planets fall into evil in Madeline L'Engle's *A Wrinkle in Time* (1962), but unlike L'Engle's Black Thing, the Evil One's cloud in *Dance of the Stones* lacks any underlying connection with events in the story to explain its spread. As in *The White Horse Talisman*, a Wise One takes a child to the past to see where the hidden magical item is. More justification for the children's involvement is given than in the first book: the Wise Ones now explain that human rituals were used to hide the objects and therefore human rituals are required to retrieve them.

Like the first in this series, the second story combines the children's quest to aid the powerful yet inexplicably helpless Wise Ones with family drama. However, aside from Adam, who remains the most fully-developed character—angry, sullen, and convinced the failure of his parents' marriage is somehow all his fault—there is little characterization. The heroes remain passive. The Wise Ones tend to solve the children's problems by telling them what to do, and what actual independent problem-solving there is often takes place "off-stage", weakening the dramatic impact of the story. Although *The Summer of Magic Quartet*, which continues with *Heart of the Hill* (2005) and *Behind the Sorcerer's Cloak* (2006), certainly does offer a story which will hold the interest of younger children who want something more imaginative than the usual "chapter books" aimed at beginning readers, the fantasy is thinly realized and fairly predictable, and the presentation of the historical elements can be misleading.

The Goodfellow Chronicles (J)

The Goodfellow Chronicles series begins with *The Sacred Seal* (2001) a first novel by picture book author and illustrator J.C. Mills. Here enchantment, present but usually unperceived in the everyday world, enters the life of an ordinary American boy, ten year-old Sam.[3] He and Jolly Goodfellow, one of "the Sage" who inspire and guide geniuses while disguised as mice, embark on a quest for a magical scroll left by a former resident in Sam's new house. Two stories are interwoven: that of Sam and Mr. Goodfellow takes place in the present, while the second, which is told to Sam by Mr. Goodfellow, is about adventures with his now-missing nephew Edgar and the "evil" Fen before the Second World War. The connections between the two storylines only begin to intersect by the end. The Fen never do anything very threatening or villainous in either time, though, with the result that most of the interest in the book lies in Sam's ongoing initiation into the ways of the Sage. There is little dramatic tension.

The Sacred Seal is followed by *The Messengers* (2002) and *The Book of the Sage* (2004). In *The Messengers*, Sam travels to England, continues searching for the missing scroll, and must find Jolly Goodfellow and Edgar, now both missing as well. The final book in the series is set many decades later. Sam, a lighthouse keeper and guardian of the two ancient scrolls recovered earlier, lives in a future where expeditions to Mars are commonplace. His

---

[3] Though written by a Canadian and published by a Canadian press, the main character and the setting of *The Sacred Seal* are American. Since the American setting plays no role in the story, perhaps the intention was to appeal to an American market; there is a perception among many twenty-first century Canadian publishers that stories with a Canadian setting (or Canadian spellings) will not sell in the United States, and that they must be, if not Americanised, at least rendered neutral, lest they offend.

alliance with the Sage continues, as the battle against the Fen draws to a climax. The expository style of the narrative is maintained to the end, with both author and characters continuing to explain, rather than taking readers emotionally into the unfolding of events.

The idea of small folk living unnoticed among humans is an enduringly appealing one in fantasy, from the diminutive fairies of the nineteenth century to Norton's *Borrowers* of the nineteen-fifties, children have been fascinated by imagining *how* such little people might exist and their way of life; *The Goodfellow Chronicles* does this very well. The ancient conflict between Sage and Fen is less developed and given less grounding than convincing fantasy demands; there is too much of a tendency to *explain* that the Fen are evil, while much of the time their actions in the story make them appear merely moderately troublesome. They are fit opponents for a ten-year-old, not the threat to the destiny of the human race that Jolly Goodfellow insists they are. The story claims to be relating conflict on an epic scale, while never moving out of the mode of a child's adventures with a magical mentor-creature in a formerly unperceived magical underlayer of the everyday world. Though the latter has a rich and venerable tradition in fantasy writing, the failure of the Sage and Fen to live up to the weighty roles in which they are cast leaves the story hanging unconvincingly between the two types of tale. Characters involved in fateful conflicts may be comic and the whole story the richer for it, but they must also have the force, the depth, to live up to the demands their roles place upon them, and in this series, neither heroes nor villains move convincingly into those roles. They never convince the reader that the fate of the world is bound up with their actions or the outcome of the conflict between them.

The Maze (YA)

Monica Hughes, who died in 2003, is regarded as the grande dame of Canadian children's speculative fiction, famous particularly for her excellent *Isis* science fiction trilogy of the early eighties, although she wrote a large number of juvenile science fiction and realistic adventure books over the course of her long career. *The Maze* (2002) is among her last works. The heroine, Andrea Austin, lives with her misogynistic, controlling father. Her mother has left the family because she could not cope with her husband continually putting her down, but does not seem to have felt any need to guard her daughter against similar psychological abuse. Andrea, in the early twenty-first century, is expected to dress like a girl of the nineteen-fifties and do all the work of a housewife while maintaining high grades. In her new school she is bullied and swarmed by a gang led by Crystal. Hiding in an antique store, Andrea thinks of Nesbit's *The Story of the Amulet* (1906) and wishes there really were such things as magic amulets. The store's owner, Sofia, promptly offers her tea and a magic box, which is able to take her into a maze. Andrea does not explore this, however. Later, Crystal and her follower Sabrina open the box and are zapped into the maze. The police investigating the missing girls, after hearing Andrea's description of their attack on her, say, "You really have a grudge against the girls, don't you?"[4] This disturbing assumption of the victim's complicity in her abuse passes unchallenged and unquestioned.

    Andrea only enters the maze some days later, after Sofia tells her that she must, to rescue the trapped girls and find a powerful stone located at its centre, though what the stone can do once found is left unexplained. (Perhaps for a sequel that was never written?) She finds that Crystal, a foster child with psychological problems, is controlling the reality of the maze, creating worlds of violence. Breaking with Crystal, Sabrina creates her own place where she sits calmly under a bush, indulges in a little self-analysis, and instantly reforms. Andrea finds Crystal, survives the girl's attempts to injure or kill her in various hostile worlds, and finally starts to feel sympathy for the antagonistic bully. They find the centre and the stone, collect Sabrina, and return to the real world a week in the past, apparently preventing the disappearance of Crystal and Sabrina from having happened. Are there two Andreas at this point in time? The book does not examine the possibility. Andrea simply gets Crystal's advice on changing her wardrobe and hairstyle, and tracks down her mother for a visit.

    As fantasy, the whole book is very contrived. The heroine wishes she had a magic amulet and is promptly given a magical item, the sole purpose of which is to change her life by helping her

---

[4] Hughes, *The Maze*, p. 45.

work through a problem. It is impossible to believe in the reality of such a coincidence, lacking any connection with anything else in the story to weave it naturally into the plot. Although the plot has superficial similarities to Ende's *The Neverending Story* (1979; 1983 in English translation) it is far weaker in execution. In *The Neverending Story*, Bastian may be meant by some power within Fantastica to be the one who takes the book which enables him to enter the world; he may be destined to be the hero who either saves the world and incidentally himself, or by betraying himself fails, but no-one tells him, "Take it, it's good for you, you will learn how to be a Better Boy if you undergo this prescribed experience." *The Maze* seems designed to teach a number of lessons, starting with "be kind to bullies" and "if you are bullied, you brought it on yourself by being different" and concluding with "conformity is the answer to your problems". The fantasy here is mere window-dressing, a convenience having no foundation to root it within the story or to give the box and its maze any kind of history. It exists solely to teach Andrea, Crystal, and Sabrina a lesson.

The Willowmere Chronicles (YA)

Alison Baird has written fantasy for all ages, from the excellent short children's novel *The Dragon's Egg* (1994) to the adult *Dragon Throne* trilogy which began with *The Stone of the Stars* (2004). However, between that novel for young children and her breakthrough into the American adult market, she wrote for teens (see also page 94). *The Witches of Willowmere* (2002), the first in Baird's second young adult series, introduces Claire Norton, a high school student in southern Ontario who is troubled by nightmares and waking dreams; in some of these she experiences episodes in the life of a seventeenth-century Scotswoman drowned for witchcraft. Claire has no fascination with the supernatural, unlike some of the "in" crowd at her school, who, having found the local Wiccan community a boring crowd of adult "granolas", turn to the "Dark Circle" which promises them power over others. By the end of the book, Claire accepts that she is a shaman and the reincarnation of Alice Ramsay, and has reconnected with Alice's daimon or guardian spirit, Leo. She remains, though, dedicated to reasoning and researching her way through problems; this is how she discovers the truth and defeats her enemy, the aspiring teen-witch Josie.

The conflict between the malevolent daimons guiding the Dark Circle's leader and the more benevolent daimons such as Leo is also an ancient war between shamans. Claire's victory at the end of the book is only a triumph in the first skirmish. The second book, *The Warding of Willowmere* (2004), expands Claire's knowledge of her own past lives in Scotland and Africa and the battles she and Leo have fought against the shaman Mamba and his daimon familiar Phobetor through three widely-spaced lifetimes. It also continues to develop Claire as a complex and believable teenager, coping with a difficult family situation (her mother abandoned the family years before) and the usual problems of an outsider among the high school cliques. The third book, *Wyrd of Willowmere* (2005), brings Claire's and Leo's centuries-old conflict with Mamba and Phobetor to a satisfying conclusion, as well as developing further the subplots of her missing mother and the love stories past and present that entered the story in book two.

Although Claire is initially a very unhappy person, this is not used as a simplistic method of presenting a typical teen protagonist; from the start there is more to Claire than her unhappiness, and she is not shown wallowing in it, but continually struggling to remain engaged with the world beyond her own problems. She proves a strong and resilient hero, both thoughtful and reflective, and an active mover in the unfolding plot. The discussions of Wicca as a modern belief assembled in the nineteen-fifties are interesting and accurate, a corrective to occasional New Age claims of an unbroken European pagan tradition. Baird's writing has achieved maturity; the slight flavour of convenience underlying her earlier book *The Hidden World* (see page 94)—in which the adventure sometimes seemed provided as a distraction from reality and a *means* of forcing the protagonist to mature—has been left behind. In *The Willowmere Chronicles*, high school and family drama, and the fantasy elements of reincarnation, warning dreams, and daimon familiars are fully integrated, working together to create a rich and believable literary reality.

The Blue Girl (YA)

Charles de Lint is one of Canada's few internationally-recognized fantasy writers. His novels and short stories are published primarily as adult fiction, but like most fantasy and science fiction, are also read by many teens. Early in his career he wrote a few secondary world fantasies such as *The Riddle of the Wren* (1984) and *The Harp of the Grey Rose* (1985) which suffered the flaws of so many late seventies/early eighties adult novels in the genre, the worst being cardboard, stock-parts worlds and characters, with numerous places, enemies, and creatures named but given no concrete reality. (Children's secondary world fantasy of the era was generally of a much higher quality.) Both these books were re-issued for teens in 2002 and 2004 respectively. In *Wolf Moon* (1988; re-issued 2004), the story of a young man who becomes a werewolf, de Lint began to develop worlds with a more solid foundation. He would go on from *Wolf Moon* to build rich, believable, and complex fantasy worlds, usually ones in which the edges of the primary world and the world of the supernatural overlap, allowing interaction between the two for a fortunate, or unfortunate, few. Most of these stories were published for adults, but *The Dreaming Place* (1990) was initially brought out as a young adult book. Its story of cousins haunted by manifestations of a Celtic and Native American Otherworld, with thoroughly believable characters and a rich fantasy capable of sustaining the reader's literary belief, shows de Lint at his best; it also was re-issued in 2002. *Waifs and Strays* (2002) is a collection of previously published short stories in which all the main characters are teens.

The Blue Girl (2004) is a young adult novel set in Newford, a city which appears in many of de Lint's adult novels and short stories. Newford is a modern North American metropolis in which the border between the human and the Otherworld (largely but not entirely founded on Celtic traditions) is thin, allowing much interaction. The hero of *The Blue Girl* is a newcomer to the city, Imogene Yeck, an independent, tough, and free-spirited girl who starts off the school year by making friends with Maxine, one of the school rejects, and refusing to be cowed by the bullies. Adrian, a ghost who haunts the school, falls in love with her for her independence and integrity. Though Imogene befriends him, she cannot see the fairies—rogue hobs or brownies—who in life and afterlife have been his only friends and who deliberately caused his death, a mere prank, so far as they were concerned. Adrian's attempts to make her able to see more of the Otherworldly beings draw the attention of the anamithim, which some call soul-eaters. Imogene, her childhood imaginary friend Pelly, and Maxine research the fairies and anamithim and try to find a way to save Imogene, though even the angel John Narraway believes anyone the anamithim go after is doomed. Adrian, too, tries to find ways to save Imogene, once he is convinced of his own responsibility for her situation. All three teens, living and dead, discover new strength and maturity through the course of their year-long struggle. The story unfolds with a great deal of humour, drama, action, and thoughtfulness, in elegant and readable prose. The intermingling of sections in past and present tense, from different narrative perspectives, works very well. De Lint's Newford is one of the significant fantasy worlds of the turn of the millennium and *The Blue Girl* is an outstanding story from it.

The Chronicles of Faerie (J/YA)

O.R. Melling's first two novels for young readers, *The Druid's Tune* (CLA Young Adult Canadian Book Award 1984) and *The Singing Stone*, were re-issued in 2003 and 2004 respectively. Both tell stories of young people drawn, not into the historical past, but into an Ireland of legend and myth. However, it is with *The Chronicles of Faerie* that Melling came into her own. *The Chronicles of Faerie* has had several incarnations and may be found on library shelves in various editions. Originally published as *The Hunter's Moon* (1993), *The Summer King* (1999), *The Light-Bearer's Daughter* (2001), and *The Book of Dreams* (2003), the first three books were re-issued in one volume as *The Chronicles of Faerie* (2002). Melling then revised *The Hunter's Moon*, expanding and deepening it. This revised second edition was published separately in the United States (2005) and is the version included in *The Golden Book of Faerie*, which contains all four books in the series (2004). A revised and expanded second edition of *The Summer King* was published in the United States as well (2006), to be followed a revised second edition of *The Light-Bearer's Daughter* (2007).

Each of Melling's books in this series features a contemporary protagonist facing some trouble in her own life, who must undertake a quest on behalf of Faerie in order both to prevent some great disaster of which she is at first only vaguely aware, and to win something she herself greatly desires. Melling's Faerie is the world of Irish myth, legend, and fairy-lore. Her main characters, Gwen, Laurel, and Dana, are strong, intelligent, and must overcome external opposition as well as their own fears and failings in the course of their quests. The plots of the first three books deal with upheavals in what might be called the political aspect of the fairy world: imbalances in power and tensions among the Fairies or the old Irish gods.

In the first, Canadian Gwen searches for her cousin Findabhair, who is (very willingly) carried off to be a fairy king's love, but who will end up a sacrificial victim if Gwen and the companions she gathers on her journey around Ireland fail to save her. The story reveals that the movement between Faerie and the human world is not all one way, and not all deaths lead to the same afterlife. In the second, Laurel's sister Honor, who died on a visit to their grandparents in Ireland, has become the bride of another fairy king. Laurel is recruited for a dangerous mission to prevent the mortal and fairy worlds from drifting apart. Her quest is further complicated by a troubled young man, Ian; he is an aspect of the imprisoned Summer King, who caused Honor's death. Past and present connect, as Laurel discovers her grandfather's youthful involvement in the Summer King's imprisonment for the killing of the Queen of the Eagles. In the second edition of *The Summer King*, Laurel's desire to avenge her sister, the love and hate she feels for Ian, and Ian's own struggle to subdue and master the Summer King make for a rich and passionate story, perhaps the strongest of the four.

In *The Light-Bearer's Daughter*, the hero is a younger girl, not yet a teen. Dana, upset at her Canadian father's decision to take her back to Canada, is sent by the fairy queen Honor to carry a vital message to another fairy king, Lugh, a message that only she has any chance of delivering because of a connection to Faerie of which she is unaware. Her journey across modern, historical, and mythical Ireland unravels the mystery of the mother who disappeared years before, and as in the first two books, both the

Faerie and the human worlds are affected by the outcome of the girl's mission.

In *The Book of Dreams*, Melling surpassed herself, demanding more of her storytelling, and this inspired the revision of the previous three books in the series. Longer, more complex, and more fully-realized in detail than the original editions of the first three novels, *The Book of Dreams* continues Dana's story in a Canadian setting. Dana's quest to prevent servants of a nihilistic force that hates all life from severing the worlds of humanity and Faerie, thus destroying both, takes her from coast to coast to coast. Dana resents her family having moved from fairy-entwined Ireland to Canada, which, like the heroine of Lunn's T*he Shadow in Hawthorn Bay*, she believes to be empty of the supernatural. She feels she has been cut off from her otherworldly heritage. To save Faerie she is forced to discover the magic inherent to Canada's landscape and peoples.

The Book of Dreams is the only one of *The Chronicles of Faerie* to have a Canadian setting. The fantasy is rooted in the land and the folklore of Canada; it could be compared to Patricia Wrightson's *Book of Wirrun* trilogy in what it tries to do. Even in books like Baird's *The Hidden Land* or Slade's *Northern Frights* series, where traditional folklore comes into Canada, that folklore is not made part of Canada; it remains immigrant. In *The Book of Dreams*, Melling acknowledges other authors who write with an awareness of both European and aboriginal interpretations of the Canadian landscape. Author Sharon Butala makes a cameo appearance, while the works of Charles de Lint are discussed enthusiastically by some of the characters. De Lint pioneered the writing of fantasy set in urban, contemporary Canada, in which both mythological and folkloric beings from New and Old World cultures play prominent roles. The Canada of his fantasy is one in which ancient European gods and supernatural creatures came along with European immigrants, and settled in alongside the aboriginal supernatural pantheons. Stan Rogers, in his song "The Giant," also suggests the immigration and naturalization of Celtic mythological beings; his transplanting of the giant Fingal to Cape Breton is adopted by Melling, who refers to and builds on the works of all three of these artists in creating the Canadian supernatural discovered by Dana.

Irish fairy lore continues to be prominent in *The Book of Dreams*, but the Loup Garou and the demon-propelled flying canoe of Québecois folklore are given a new life. There are Chinese guardian dragons in Toronto's Chinatown, the Hindu god Ganesh appears, Fingal lives in Cape Breton and is romancing the British sea-spirit Mother Carey. There are hard-partying goblins in Cape Breton, trolls in a parallel system of tunnels beneath Toronto's subway, and clans of fairies who emigrated with the Irish and are as Canadian as anyone else whose ancestors came over one or two centuries ago. Of central importance are the Old Ones, who are the spirits honoured by the aboriginal peoples. These are the great powers of Turtle Island, the New World. In addition to these ancient spirits from Inuit and other native mythologies, Melling's book is peopled with modern aboriginal shamans and passing heroes who might be ordinary men or might be semi-supernatural champions, between the mortal and the supernatural world just as Dana and her shapeshifting boyfriend Jean are.

Melling deals well with family relationships both contented and troubled, and her stories always maintain a hope for balance and reconciliation, although the resolutions are never simple. Her Faerie is built on a foundation of Irish fairy traditions and mythology. Melling's fairies are driven by their own codes of conduct, their own desires; they do not exist for the gratification of those humans who are drawn into their world, and involvement with them can have a terrible cost. However, she presents the human and the Otherworld as mutually dependent and interwoven. In *The Book of Dreams*, and in the revised second editions of *The Hunter's Moon, The Summer King*, and *The Light-Bearer's Daughter*, Melling sets Canadian children's fantasy a new standard for encounters between modern heroes and traditional folklore and mythology.

The Bone Flute (J)

Although Patricia Bow has written a number of children's fantasies, nearly all her books have had their only publication in German translation in Germany; *The Bone Flute* (2004) was only her second book to be published in English, seven years after her first.

The Bone Flute draws on the Orpheus motif found throughout European folktales, which tells of a man or woman trying to win back a lost love from otherworldly or magical captivity. In Bow's story, a bard, Diarmid, loses his bride, Rhianna, to Gwyn, son of the lord of the Otherworld. With a flute made from the leg bone of an Otherworldly dog, Diarmid pulls Rhianna back across the river of time, only to lose her again. Camrose, a modern girl, is a Keeper charged with finding the flute and choosing its true owner; failing to make a choice will have fatal consequences for her family. Both Gwyn and Diarmid claim the flute, but Camrose gives it up to Gwyn's red hound, whose leg-bone it is. The hound, revealed as Rhianna, is released to experience the life she was denied, without having to accept either of the men who desire to possess her.

Although the first chapters of the story are well-written and suspenseful, and the story continues to be dramatic and intriguing to the end, the characters of Camrose and her supernatural helper Miranda, and the themes concerned with ancient wrongs, obsessions, and individual freedom, lack depth. None of the characters develop over the course of the story, or, in the case of Diarmid and Gwyn, over their long pursuit and harassment of the Keepers. Despite Camrose's convenient discovery of an ability for out-of-body flight in the last chapter, there has been no real transformation or growth on the part of any of the dominant characters.

Moreover, there is confusion as to whether it was Gwyn or the Wyrde, the three Fates, who turned Rhianna into the red hound, and whether or not Gwyn knew all along that the hound was Rhianna. If he knew and was in fact the one who transformed her, why could he not turn her back? Since she was Gwyn's hound before her leg was cut off and has appeared to Diarmid as a woman since, why is the missing bone the critical element to transform and free her? Or, if it was the Wyrde who transformed Rhianna to hide her, as is suggested at another point, what was the purpose of the Keepers? In the end it is an easy matter for the Wyrde to set Rhianna free. This makes it appear that it was their choice to turn Rhianna into a hound and leave her in Gwyn's power, though she did nothing to promote the conflict between the men. The victim is cruelly punished; no reason appears in the story for Rhianna's long suffering and enslavement as a dog except the whim of the Wyrde, who *do* act to determine what will happen despite repeated statements to the contrary. They are not shown to be the distant and disinterested weavers of fate which the book proclaims them to be; they are active players, judging and assigning punishments, asking people what they want and gratifying that desire, admonishing. Overall, even though the story is fantasy for its own sake and had the potential to be a strong work, the logic of the foundation and the initiating event of the plot is flawed, preventing the book from being consistently convincing in its reality and achieving all it otherwise might have.

Wolf Pack (J)

Wolf Pack (2004) is the first in a series by adult horror and speculative fiction author and editor Edo van Belkom, who has also written some horror for teens. This story of four modern teens growing up in the British Columbia interior begins when forest ranger Garrett Brock adopts four orphaned wolf cubs who turn out to be werewolves. Noble, Argus, Harlan, and Tora Brock attend school and have all the problems of normal teenagers, with a few extra difficulties thrown in. A scientist filming a documentary on forest fires captures their transformation into wolf form on tape. Dreaming of fame on the talk-show circuit, Dr. Monk sets a trap and catches Tora.

When their father's attempt to free the "wolf" by legal means fails, the boys set out to rescue their sister themselves. In the course of their mission, they face the ethical issues posed by the inhuman strength of their half-human, half-wolf form, as well as their desire for revenge against Monk and his film crew. In the end the brothers resist the temptation to kill their sister's abductor and settle for destroying the tapes and letting Monk make a public fool of himself.

Wolf Pack won the 2005 Aurora Award for best English long form speculative fiction work, as well as the 2006 Silver Birch Award. It is well-paced and well-plotted with lots of action, which is balanced with the ability of the heroes to reason out the consequences of their actions and plan ahead. Characterization is realistic as far as it goes, but remains quite shallow throughout. Tora is overlooked for much of the story, her function merely to be captured. She is passive and helpless, patiently waiting for rescue; her feelings and actions as a prisoner hardly touched on.

In the sequel, *Lone Wolf* (2005) van Belkom continues to explore the difficulties faced by the siblings, caught between two worlds, completely at home and accepted in neither. Argus's urge to leave his family and return to the wild, where werewolves still live in secret, is combined with a plot focussing on the complex political and environmental issues surrounding modern forestry. Although characterization and character growth remain the story's weak point (even Argus is not developed beyond the identifying character traits provided in the first book), the fantasy element is well executed. Van Belkom portrays in a convincing manner the problems the siblings face in high school due to their unusual human appearances, while adding depth to the fantasy by glimpses of the "wild" werewolves and their society.

MORE "ACCESSIBLE" THAN SOME types of fantasy for readers not immersed in the genre, though enduringly popular with dedicated fantasy readers, primary world fantasy is vulnerable to being used in a shallow or derivative way. There are still authors and publishers who seem willing to "mystic up" an uninspired everyday story, or one lacking the attention to internal consistency and logic which any and every genre of literature requires, with the careless introduction of a few generic fantasy or paranormal elements, as though calling it fantasy excuses poor literary quality. Just as with secondary world fantasy, works in which the story and the fantasy are shallow or ill-conceived continue to be published on the strength of their apparent novelty.

On the whole, however, in fantasy set in the primary world, Canadian books at the dawn of the twenty-first century show an improvement. Some of the strongest Canadian fantasy writing in the period 2000-2004 is primary world fantasy. Both Melling and de Lint, who can be counted among the best Canadian authors writing for young people today, write fantasy in which the fantastic intersects with the lives of contemporary real-world protagonists. Works like *The Witches of Willowmere*, *The Loki Wolf*, and *Wolf Pack* display an ability on the part of other Canadian writers to create strong stories in which fantasy is an integral part of the world, thoroughly believable and never a mere device, convenience, or novelty decoration.

IV
SPECULATIVE FANTASY

ALL FANTASY IS BY ITS NATURE speculative, founded on imaginative considerations of "what if..." Both fantasy and science fiction are encompassed within the broader term "speculative fiction", and as with any attempt to categorize things as individual as books, a continuum of works bridges any categories that can be created. There exists fantasy with elements of science fiction; science fiction with elements of fantasy.

Science fiction can be defined as speculative fiction based on scientific possibilities, or extrapolations from contemporary technologies and knowledge. Jules Verne, for instance, wrote science fiction in the second half of the nineteenth century considering "what ifs" based on the technology and scientific speculation of his day, giving us such works as *From the Earth to the Moon* (1865) and *20,000 Leagues Under the Sea* (1870). A recent Canadian example of science fiction for young readers is Troon Harrison's *Eye of the Wolf* (2003).[1] The story of Chandra Singh's search for her kidnapped mother is set in a world based on current scientific speculation, examining the effects of a human-induced ice age on culture and politics at both the local and the global level. The technology is plausibly extrapolated from today's and adapted to the future circumstance of a country short of food and fuel and under eight metres of snow. The society portrayed, from the government-regulated communal life necessitated by the dictates of survival, to the rapacious gangs of anarchist Snow Warriors who react against this, is rationally constructed. In its portrayal of future society, technology, and the state of the environment, the book does what good science fiction should do: it promotes consideration of humanity's potential and current course, of possibilities good and bad to be worked towards or avoided, and it casts a

---

[1] More recently, although after the time-period covered in this study, Harrison has begun an extremely good young adult secondary world fantasy series, *Tales of Terre*, with *The Separated* (2006) and *The Twilight Box* (2007).

light on aspects of our current society that sometimes slip by us unnoticed. Janet McNaughton's *The Secret Under My Skin* (2000) and *The Raintree Rebellion* (2006) are likewise science fiction, depicting a twenty-fourth-century future in a thought-provoking manner while telling a compelling story.

Eye of the Wolf, *The Secret Under My Skin*, and *The Raintree Rebellion* are clearly science fiction, not fantasy, but other recent books are less easy to categorize, containing elements of science fiction and of fantasy. Such works may take speculation about the nature of the universe or such established science fiction motifs as parallel worlds and alien (but not supernatural) lifeforms, or technological advances, or environmental change, and combine them with fantasy elements such as magical powers and supernatural (rather than merely alien) beings. Jules Verne's *Journey to the Centre of the Earth* (1864) might be considered to blend elements of fantasy and science fiction; many of Diana Wynne Jones' books, with their parallel worlds and powerful, technologically advanced peoples, could also be counted as speculative fantasy. *A Tale of Time City* (1987), in which a Second World War London evacuee is kidnapped through a case of mistaken identity and taken to the city that monitors the course of history, *The Homeward Bounders* (1981) in which a boy spies on alien beings who play games with human lives and is condemned to wander multiple worlds forever, and *Hexwood*'s combination of a cosmos-spanning empire, androids, Merlin, Arthur, and dragons (1993) are good examples of recent speculative fantasy by Jones. Australian Garth Nix's *Shade's Children* (1997), in which a resistance group of children combats seven Overlords from another dimension who have destroyed all adults and are harvesting children's minds to run cyborgs for a ritualistic battle game, is a work even more capable of being classed on the science fiction end of the speculative fiction spectrum, particularly given its setting, the post-apocalyptic ruins of our civilization. It could also be considered to contain elements of fantasy. The Overlords and their means of crossing dimensions and causing all adults to suddenly vanish remain mysterious to the heroes, who even in the end are unable discover how the alien devices work; an element of mystery, even of possible magic, suffuses the Overlords' deepest secrets.

However, no twentieth-century Canadian fantasies that could

belong to this subgenre are discussed by Egoff or Saltman, though the fact that works which feature a future setting, futuristic details, or the pseudo-scientific paranormal of ESP and telekinesis are often marketed by publishers as science fiction may sometimes lead to their exclusion from discussions of fantasy. Leaving aside primary world stories drawing on pop culture paranormal, in Canada, books blurring the boundaries between fantasy and science fiction, between magic and science, are a relatively new phenomenon.

Dust (J/YA)

Dust (2001), by Arthur Slade (who as Arthur G. Slade wrote the *Northern Frights* trilogy, see page 43), won both the Saskatchewan Book Award and the Governor-General's Literary Award. *Dust* is, in its components, similar to the novels of John Bellairs, such as *The Curse of the Blue Figurine* (1983): a story which evokes a particular time and place in careful detail, with the protagonist a boy confronting an ancient, malevolent force to which the adults in his life are largely oblivious. In *Dust*, eleven-year-old Robert is the only one to recognize and oppose effectively a soulless immortal, Harsich, who kidnaps children, including Robert's brother, in order to extract their souls, which he offers to a race of aliens or demons in return for a soul of his own. Why these beings want the children's souls is never explained. They are not developed in any detail, but neither is their mystery conveyed in such a way as to render them intriguing or frightening. Instead, they appear almost an afterthought, a justification for Harsich's actions imposed from outside rather than growing naturally out of the story. Harsich's devices for bringing rain to the drought-stricken community and for extracting souls also lack integration into the wider world of the story or with the tormented past which Harsich claims as the justification for his actions. They seem a convenience, lacking the history that would make them real.

Slade's writing in this novel lacks the touch of humour that gives Bellairs' stories life and warmth, and which is present in Slade's own *Northern Frights* series. Compared to *Northern Frights*, *Dust* feels flat, lacking the earlier series' emotional range from tragedy to joy. The strongest element in the story is the portrayal of Robert, an overlooked eldest son who saves not only his younger brother but the adult authorities who should have been protecting the town. The relationship between the demons or aliens and Harsich never quite convinces, however, because it is never shown as an ongoing, developing situation influencing Harsich and his actions; it is introduced quite suddenly at the crisis of the story. As a result, the fantasy itself is never entirely believable, and seems contrived as a way of explaining things at the end, similar to the mystery novel detective who summons the suspects to the drawing room and presents them with evidence of the murderer's guilt based on clues the author has neglected to provide for the reader. Such rabbit-out-of-hat solutions rarely count as good literary plotting in any genre. That the book garnered attention not usually accorded Canadian children's fantasy may in part be due to its acceptability as "Canlit"; it has the correct ingredients (rural prairie community, the Depression, the Boy repressed by religious family) to be classed as "literature" rather than "genre" by those who regard the two terms as mutually exclusive and the second as derogatory. At the same time, its fantasy elements of demonic aliens and a magical soul-extracting machine, despite being so superficially inserted into the story, are a novelty in a "lit" fiction.

The Mole Wars (J)

J. Fitzgerald McCurdy's *The Fire Demons* (2004), first in her series *The Mole Wars*, is a very conventional "magic in the primary world" fantasy, except that both the evil and good characters with magical powers are described as aliens. Their attributes, though, are those of stock demons and wizards. *The Fire Demons* begins with a bullied boy in Toronto, who discovers he has a part to play in an ancient battle against "alien terrorists" who came from another galaxy to destroy all life on the planet of the Mages. These "terrorists" are described as unintelligent, operating solely on instinct; how a mere animal can have developed interstellar travel and become capable of fighting a war lasting eight centuries is never explained. Long before the book begins, the Mages, using an "ancient globe" with no further provenance or attributes, had destroyed most of the enemy. The survivors were imprisoned in a newly-forming planet, the Earth, with Wardens sent to guard them. However, the prisoners turned into creatures of fire and escaped, becoming Fire Demons; when the story opens they are kidnapping children and taking their memories. This is part of their plan to escape, readers are told, though not why they need to do this, having already escaped. The hero of the book, Steele, is recruited by the Mage Maddie Fey to help find the missing children. Though he is told he is actually a Mage, Steele has little role to play; his presence is largely incidental to the action, as a passive observer rather than a precipitator of events. The plotting and literary style show no improvement over McCurdy's earlier *The Serpent's Egg* trilogy (see page 95); readers are told what emotion characters are supposed to be feeling but are never shown them reacting to events in any convincing way. The audience is never taken into a character's emotional or psychological reality.

Although there is no reason not to write a fantasy about magic-using extra-terrestrials, and many authors for children and adults have done so, McCurdy's fantasy elements and aliens both fail to be believable; internal logic and the coherency and consistency of the world are never established. A species with only animal will, lacking sentience, cannot be terrorist in philosophy and cannot wage war (and is extremely unlikely to stumble upon a means of interplanetary travel). The Fire Demons have either escaped or are preparing to escape, readers are told in different places; the means by which children's memories can fuel an escape is not even hinted at, and neither is the reason for children rather than adults to be taken. Like so much else, it is stated as fact, to be accepted by the reader. Neither Mages nor Fire Demons are developed in any detail; their societies and conflict presented as merely "good" and "evil", labels readers are supposed to accept without evidence. The overall effect of this is a world and characters which cannot sustain literary belief. All speculative fiction demands rigorous attention to the created reality, and that rigour is lacking here. Even though the fantasy is the foundation of the plot, it has no more substance than a veneer. Moreover, the style is laboured and juvenile, characterized by overblown and inapt similes. Though the superficial novelty may attract a young audience with little previous literary experience, it is a book unlikely to travel onwards with a growing mind. Fantasy literature and literature for children, like any other forms of literature, require good writing to be good books.

The Longlight Legacy (YA)

The Dirt Eaters (2003) is the first in a trilogy called *The Longlight Legacy*, by Dennis Foon. Foon is a prolific playwright who specializes in dramas for a teen audience, often dealing with difficult issues; he has also written novels with similar themes, but the trilogy *The Longlight Legacy* is his first venture into fantasy. The series is set in a post-apocalyptic future, the origins of which most of the characters no longer know. Later references to a river poisoned by the bombing of a chemical plant and to a genocide enable readers to deduce that the civilization-destroying event in the past, called simply "the Madness", was probably a global war.

The hero, Roan, is a teenage boy from the village of Longlight, which tries to live peacefully, preserving historical memories of the Madness and some elements of past technology, such as solar power. They are pacifists and vegetarians, working to restore the poisoned land. Roan and his sister Stowe are the only people of Longlight to survive a massacre, but Stowe is abducted by the leaders of the Clans that run the City and prey on the countryside. Roan spends time with the Brothers, a group of warriors following a religion created by Saint, their illiterate leader, from pictures of Mithras in books of Classical history; though Roan learns to fight, he discovers the Brothers were the killers of his village and flees after an unsuccessful attack on Saint. His journey eventually bring him to the Forgotten of Oasis, a community peaceful but not pacifist, which, like Longlight, preserves what was good of the past. He and his friend Lumpy also rescue a group of children whose own town is selling them for their organs. Thus far, the story could be science fiction, but Roan's dreams of talking animals and animal-human chimeras turn out to be not mere dreams but a mystic skill, Dreamwalking, which is for most of its practitioners facilitated by eating a particular clay, hence the title. As well, it becomes apparent that Roan is the focus of various prophecies. However, much about Roan, his world, and his destiny remains to be discovered in the subsequent books.

Freewalker (2004) resumes the story some months later. Roan, Lumpy, and the children have founded a new settlement called Newlight. When the children all fall into comas simultaneously, Roan and Lumpy, not entirely trusting the Dirt Eaters, who may have their own plans for Roan and the children, set out to find some way to save the children themselves. Roan discovers that four groups were originally established to oppose Darius, leader of the City and Stowe's captor. Longlight was one, Oasis another. A third, the Gunthers, who maintain the infrastructure of the City while working against Darius, become allies in Roan's attempts to enter the City. The fourth are a secret community of warrior women.

The narrative alternates between Roan and his sister Stowe. She is made a Dirt Eater by her captors, becomes addicted, and is trained to fight and to kill in the Dreamfields, becoming an assassin for the City, a weapon against the Dirt Eaters. She is presented in propaganda as "Our Stowe", a saintly icon of the fascist City. But she knows it was the Masters of the City who had the Brothers massacre Longlight, and she keeps a corner of her mind to herself. Stowe evades Roan when he comes to rescue her, fearing he may come between her and her vengeance.

Freewalker brings in more technology of the past and revelations about the evolving nature of humans and animals since the apocalypse. We learn more about the competing societies, particularly about the City, which is not merely a totalitarian city-state preying upon the countryside, but a fascist distopia; the Masters of the City use devices called Enablers to control the populace, turning most of them into tractable workers no longer capable of independent thought and emotion. Many people seem to accept Enablers willingly, an interesting bit of allegorical social criticism.

By the end, Roan learns more about his past and his destiny, coming to terms with his abandonment of the pacifist philosophy of Longlight. He faces the future and what he must do, trying to become the leader he seems destined to be, the person who has the potential to bring change. Stowe, meanwhile, has escaped the City; she nearly surrenders to Enabling, and is almost incapacitated by her Dirt addiction. The story becomes more mythic in tone and concludes in *The Keeper's Shadow* (2006), in which Roan, Lumpy, and Stowe continue their various battles against Darius, the Keeper of the City, bringing the possibility of renewal to the land.

The setting of *The Longlight Legacy*, both its post-apocalyptic future and the fantasy aspect of the Dreamwalkers and the dreamworld in which they meet, is detailed and convincing. Foon has obviously put much thought developing his grim future. He does not merely recycle the stage-dressing from the post-World War Three movies of the seventies and eighties, but works to create hierarchical, interlocked societies feeding off one another, in a world where law to protect the weak and the authority to enforce it have not yet been re-established. Roan is a thoughtful, intelligent, reasoning hero as well as a physically adept one. He is active, not reactive; he thinks situations through, makes plans, and has long-term strategies. The one factor that works against complete belief in the story is the present-tense narrative. People do not experience life all in the present tense except in moments of extreme concentration: battle, fear, dream. An entire complex story told in the present can make for a cold and distancing read, whereas we ought to be deeply and passionately rooted in Roan's perspective. The reader is reduced to an outside observer, not carried into Roan's experience of time as a more conventional narrative able to use past, imperfect and pluperfect as well as present might have done. However, *The Longlight Legacy* is a very good story and very good fantasy literature.

Flux and *Fixed* (YA)

Beth Goobie's *Flux* (2004) is set in an alternate world, which is a departure for Goobie, a very prolific novelist for teens; although a number of her books include the paranormal, the setting is usually contemporary North America and the protagonist a troubled teen. *Flux* and its sequel *Fixed* move between alternate worlds or layers of existence, but none are recognizably our own. The world in *Flux* is divided into two societies, the totalitarian Interior and the more anarchic Outbacks. Nellie Joan Kinnan, a twelve year-old orphan in the Outbacks, has the ability to travel through what she thinks of as levels, closely connected realities, in which she has doubles. Nellie and gang-leader Deller, an enemy who becomes a friend, investigate the secrets of the Interior breeding programme which produced Nellie. They discover a little about the inhuman sarpa who claim to have ruled the world in the past and whose genes give people like Nellie their abilities; they also run afoul of a knife-wielding Nellie-double who knows far more about the world than either of them. Through their friendship, both characters, initially rather unpleasant personalities, develop some empathy for others and mature. Nellie and Deller take onto themselves responsibilities not only for their own actions, but for the well-being of others and their society as a whole.

In the sequel, *Fixed* (2005), the main character is Nellie Joan's twin Nellie Joanne, a commando for the Goddess Ivana who is programmed and controlled by implants in her brain. Nellie Joan and Deller try to rescue Nellie's twin and Deller's younger brother, but their quest has tragic consequences. Despite this, Nell, as Nellie Joan becomes, is able to help Nellie Joanne rebel against her indoctrination. Nell becomes an agent for change in a society of religious totalitarianism, a *Nineteen Eighty-Four*-like world of false wars, in which the ultimate powers-that-be are the sarpas, immaterial beings who have fomented a world of hatred which it may be the destiny of Nell and Nellie to overturn.

Nellie and Deller are believable young people struggling through situations almost beyond their abilities, with their success always in doubt. Mystery and conspiracy are revealed a little at a time but at frequent intervals, in a manner likely to encourage even reluctant readers to continue eagerly. Goobie's skill with and evident enjoyment of the power of language will engage her readers, though in *Flux* some scenes, especially those describing rapid and dramatic action, seem overworked and distractingly plush; by *Fixed* the tendency to overwork such passages has lessened. *Flux* and *Fixed* take place in a thoroughly-imagined, well-created world. All the elements—the mysticism, the experiments of the Interior scientists, the contrasting but linked societies of Interior and Outbacks, and the multiple realities—work together convincingly; they are not mere backdrop but essential in the formation both of Nellie's personality and the plot. The technological and scientific elements are part of the fantasy; unlike in the pure science fiction of Harrison's *Eye of the Wolf*, these are not necessarily extrapolations from current science or scientific speculation on real possibilities, and the supernatural plays a central role. Although there is much—genetic manipulation, technological devices for mind control, and brainwashing— that has a foundation in current science or at least future possibility, gods, ghosts, and other magical beings are also a fundamental part of the world, making the story fantasy rather than science fiction.

ALTHOUGH THE COMBINING OF IDEAS from fantasy and science fiction in a pick and mix fashion can sometimes be symptomatic of sloppy world-building or unclear conception, "speculative fantasy", done with the same attention to internal consistency and logic as the creation of other fantasy plots and worlds, offers scope for unique and complex stories. Among the speculative fantasy published in Canada in the period from 2000 to 2004, Foon and Goobie stand out for their strong and intriguing novels, distinguished by their attention to the reality created as well as by good all-round storytelling. Both have used the freedom offered by the combination of science fiction and fantasy elements to explore the development of the individual in societies which echo and contrast with our own, returning to one of the basic strengths of speculative fiction, the ability to hold a mirror to the real world, throwing light into dark corners and exaggerating previously overlooked details to draw attention to them.

V
RE-IMAGININGS OF OLDER TALES

FAIRY-TALES, FOLKTALES, BALLADS, myths, and legends all contain much that is fantasy, so it is hardly surprising that they have been used as the foundations for new works by many writers. Everyone is familiar with the retelling of fairy-tales in picture book form, but retelling older stories in novels allows the writer greater freedom. Themes only hinted at in the original may be expanded to dominate the story; peripheral characters can take centre stage; the inner thoughts and hidden motivations, the complex psychology of the novel, may be brought to characters previously existing only in archetypal form. Great heroes of legend may be redrawn as flawed and suffering mortals; the monsters of fairy-tale become complex and sympathetic beings, even heroes themselves. A wide range of approaches has been taken to such retellings over the years. Andrew Lang's *Fairy Books* (1889-1910) retold tales from around the world in beautiful prose, in a form that is still the best introduction to many such stories, but he also took the familiar ballad motif of the knight held captive by the fairy queen and used it as the basis for an "historical fantasy" set in the Scottish border country, *The Gold of Fairnilee* (1888). Philip Pullman's *I Was a Rat!* (1999) takes "Cinderella" as its starting point and tells the story of one of the transformed rats who misses the end of the ball and remains trapped in human form, a small boy lost and alone in an unfamiliar and frightening world. Robin McKinley's two very different retellings of "Beauty and the Beast", *Beauty* (1978) and *Rose Daughter* (1997), her *Deerskin* (1993) and *Spindle's End* (2000), and her novel of Robin Hood, *The Outlaws of Sherwood* (1988), are further examples of the expansion of well-known tales into novels of depth and human complexity, as are the books in the fairy-tale series edited by Terri Windling. This series includes Charles de Lint's dual-world fantasy *Jack the Giant-Killer* (1990), Patricia C. Wrede's Elizabethan historical *Snow White and Rose Red* (1989), Jane Yolen's reflection on the Holocaust, *Briar Rose* (1992), and a number of others.

The art of retelling an old tale does not lie in rigid adherence to the source, but in allowing something new to grow from it.

Throughout the twentieth century, Canadian retellings of folk- and fairy-tales tended to be picture books adhering closely to their sources, or straightforward collections of folktales. French-Canadian and aboriginal stories were common subjects for such collections; none achieved the level of familiarity of Lang's *Fairy Books*, which shaped the imagination of several generations. Re-imaginings of stories into novels were almost non-existent.

The Snow Queen (YA)

Poet Eileen Kernaghan began working with traditional folklore elements in fiction in the nineties, in her novel *Dance of the Snow Dragon* (1995), which used the legends and folk-traditions of Bhutan and Tibet to tell the story of Sangay, a young Buddhist monk, the sorceress Jatsang, and their journey to the holy, hidden city of Shambhala. In *The Snow Queen* (2000), which won the 2001 Aurora Award for Canadian speculative fiction, Kernaghan's foundation is not a traditional story but one by Hans Christian Andersen first published in Danish in 1846, which until at least the mid-twentieth century was just as familiar in English as something like "Snow White" remains today. Kernaghan transforms Andersen's fairy-tale, bringing the modern novel's examination of the inner lives of the main characters to the framework of the original story. Set in nineteenth-century Scandinavia, her *Snow Queen* blends shamanism and Norse and Finnish traditions of magic with Victorian science and middle-class domestic life. Kernaghan's Gerda sets off through this world to rescue her beloved Kai from the Snow Queen, who has stolen him and frozen his heart. The book develops Gerda beyond Andersen's virtuous innocent while remaining true to the original character, and gives the reindeer-riding little robber-girl new life in Ritva, daughter of a bandit and a shaman.

Kernaghan's book looks beyond the end of Andersen's story to suggest that Gerda, who despite her unrequited love for Kai really has nothing in common with him, may herself set off in quest of further learning among the northern wise women with Ritva. This *Snow Queen* is well-crafted example of the art of retelling and re-imagining an older tale; the elements of Kernaghan's setting work naturally together, presenting a convincing reality. The fantasy here is an integral part of the story; nothing appears superficial or "made-up", and the reader is drawn into a fully believable world for the duration of the book.

After Hamelin (J)

Bill Richardson is better known as a broadcaster and author of humorous books for adults than as a children's writer, though he has written several picture books. *After Hamelin* (2000) is his only fantasy and his only children's novel. Like Kernaghan's *The Snow Queen*, *After Hamelin* retells an older story from a new perspective. The Pied Piper legend, which was recorded as far back as 1450 and given its most famous form by Robert Browning in 1842, is the novel's foundation. The narrator is a woman of 101, Penelope, and interjections from her elderly perspective are interlaced with the main narrative of herself as an eleven year-old.

Penelope's deafness saves her from being stolen by the Piper, but she sets out on a dream-journey to rescue the missing children, travelling through the world of dreams, accompanied by a cat, a Trolavian (a singing, flying, ice-dwelling creature like a long-legged troll), and an over-excitable skipping dragon. Her aim becomes not only to save the imprisoned children, but to return the Piper to the enchanted sleep into which his brother had cast him. A troubling aspect of the story is that the Piper was imprisoned for the first time before he had done anything particularly wicked; his brother merely suspected that he would, in the future, commit great wrongs because of his ability to control others with his music, which he had demonstrated but not, at that point, abused in anything but a childish way. No character within the story questions the ethics of such an act, and even within the story, the Piper's irrational malevolence seems partly attributed to his long imprisonment.

Richardson employs richer language and a more complex narrative approach in *After Hamelin* than is common in contemporary children's books; the elderly Penelope comments on her present circumstances as she writes, addressing first a reader she only imagines and then an unnamed young girl about to embark on her own adventures. This is balanced with a prose style employing short sentences and rapid action proceeding from episode to episode, as well as fairly short chapters. The fantastic element here is on the whole well integrated, although there is a degree of disjointedness about the combination of the dark fairy-tale elements of the Piper who enchants and steals children with his music, and the Trolavian and skipping dragon, who appear as superficial novelties, lacking the complexity or depth needed to make them believable as creatures existing in a world that can contain the Piper and Penelope.

An Earthly Knight (YA)

Janet McNaughton has written a number of books for children and teens. Most are historical fiction or science fiction; several have received the Ann Connor-Brimer Award for children's books. In *An Earthly Knight* (2002), which won the Newfoundland and Labrador Book Award for 2004, McNaughton takes the old Scottish ballad of "Tam Lin" as the foundation of a novel set in twelfth-century Scotland. (Her historical approach means that the novel could just as easily fit into the "historical fantasy" category which follows.) "Tam Lin" is the best-known of the class of ballads found in both Scottish and Scandinavian tradition, which tells of a knight saved, usually by a young woman, from fairy captivity and damnation. "Tam Lin" has been used as the foundation for various works of fantasy for both adults and teens over the years. Some of these, like Pamela Dean's novel *Tam Lin* (1991) in the fairy tale series edited by Terri Windling, have had a modern setting. (Dean's *Tam Lin* was re-issued for teens in 2006.) Others have moved further from the ballad while remaining recognizably related in theme, like Diana Wynne Jones' psychologically-complex *Fire and Hemlock* (1985) or Patricia A. McKillip's poetic secondary world fantasy *Winter Rose* (1996). Still others, like Lang's *The Gold of Fairnilee*, draw on the larger ballad tradition of fairy captives and rescues without reference to "Tam Lin" in particular. McNaughton combines "Tam Lin" with a second common ballad motif, that of the woman who runs away with her lover, finds he is a murderer, and kills him (or dies herself as a cautionary example). McNaughton stays close to her sources, expanding the ballad plots into a novel by adding detail, motivation and complexity in character, and fixing her story to a particular place and point in time.

Jeanette Avenel, or Jenny, is the daughter of a lord in southern Scotland. Her sister Isabel is disgraced for having run away with a knight whom she then killed in self-defence, so it falls on Jenny to make a powerful marriage for her family's benefit. Although courted by the king's brother, Earl William, she falls in love with the forest- and ruin-dwelling Tam Lin. Jenny succeeds in saving her lover from his enslavement to the fairy queen and enables her sister to find happiness with the harper Cospatric.

McNaughton's historical setting is thoroughly researched and is convincingly and accurately depicted. In a natural manner, she introduces much historical detail that may be new to young readers, making Jenny's world one which will be vividly experienced by the audience. The ballad plots and the realistic historical setting are used to examine some of the attitudes of the era to women, their status and role in the eyes of the Church and of the law, and how such official views may have been tempered in practice through affection, pragmatism, and custom. The fantasy element of the story is developed from the traditions found in the ballads and fits naturally with the historical setting. The fantasy and historical aspects are complemented by McNaughton's straightforward but elegant prose style; *An Earthly Knight* is a thoroughly convincing and absorbing fantasy.

Preposterous Fables for Unusual Children (J)

Author and illustrator Judd Palmer's series of short novels builds new stories on old tales and traditions. *The Tooth Fairy* (2002) is the least attached to a pre-existing story, taking the relatively modern tradition of the tooth fairy as its starting point. The hero of *The Tooth Fairy* is a girl, Abigail, who still has perfect baby teeth, and sets out to save the world from the Tooth Fairy, whom her grandfather, Oskar the Toothless, has taught her to fear; he sold his adult teeth in order to buy a fishing boat to support his family. The plot, for such a short book, is complex. Abigail is ruthless in using the power of her perfect teeth to charm her enemies, but it is Oskar, transformed to a bird, who saves her from the worst danger and is claimed by the Hunter, Death, who is an antlered Green Man, symbolic of the cycle of life, death, and renewal. Abigail is able to find the Tooth Fairy only because she has lost her childish self-centredness and begun to mature, but she persists in her hatred. Only when she is about to kill the Tooth Fairy does she give in to the pleas of the elderly and relent. The Tooth Fairy buys the teeth of children to make false teeth for old folks, but Oskar, in his obsessive guarding of Abigail, has cut both of them off from this cycle. Abigail, ashamed of herself, trades her perfect teeth for a set of teeth for her grandfather, even though he is dead, and "Such is the power of sacrifice for another, that Grandfather's soul halted in its passage to heaven, and was drawn back to earth. These kinds of things happen, if you didn't know".[1] The matter-of-fact miracle typifies the fairy-tale spirit of the story.

The Maestro (2002) provides the later history of the Pied Piper and the town of Hamelin after the abduction of its children. It again pits a child hero against a frightening and mysterious foe in a story of redemption and renewal. Orphaned Hannah goes to live with her aunt and uncle in Hamelin, a town where any kind of music is forbidden. Hannah is the only child in this stone-quarrying community. Musical by nature, she is exiled under pain of death when she is caught singing. She is led by the ghost of a drowned rat to the Maestro's lair within the mountains, where the Maestro, the Pied Piper, leads an orchestra composed of the stolen children, now adults, but treated as children in a not very adequate music class. The Maestro is quite mad, obsessed with wringing perfection from his orchestra: a metaphor of Art and the pursuit of the perfection that can only exist in the artist's mind. Hannah is overwhelmed by his music, but he has no use for a singer and rejects her. Her clever plan to use the Piper's charm-melody against him, to win freedom for the stolen children and a place for herself as the Maestro's student, saves not only the children, including her cousin Ludwig, but the town as well, which returns to joy, music, and cheese-making.

The series continues in the same vein with *The Wolf King* (2003), which was shortlisted for the 2004 Governor-General's Award; it examines the fable "The Boy Who Cried Wolf" in a new light. *The Sorcerer's Last Words* (2003) reinterprets and continues "The Sorcerer's Apprentice". The most recent in the series, *The Giant Killer* (2004), is again a story built on a traditional tale, that of "Jack the Giant-Killer", although as with *The Maestro*, this is

---

[1] Palmer, *The Tooth Fairy*, p. 117.

the story of what happens after the familiar story has ended.

The books in the *Preposterous Fables* series have the qualities of an oral tale, intimate and immediate. The third person narrator is old-fashioned and assertive, a dominating personality in the story even though not a character. The stories are full of humour, much of it created by the narrator's wry observations on the characters and their actions and motivations. They are also very visual books; although entire scenes are not described, a few details will be emphasized in such a way as to bring the whole to life. They have been performed as puppet plays by Palmer's Alberta-based Old Trout Puppet Workshop and the way description is used seems to resemble the arts of stage dressing and costuming: a part is cleverly used to suggest the whole, as when the Hunter's fruit-bearing antlers convey the whole mysterious, ominous, and ever-living person of Death and the cycle of life. Palmer also has a knack for the unexpected phrase that makes the reader see things anew: "Hannah fled into the enormous night".[2] "'This is Art, child. You may want it. But that is irrelevant. The question is: Does Art want you?'"[3] "The music reached the glowing embers of God's heart, and then floated back to earth ...".[4] The stories in the series are idiosyncratic, charming, delightful, and thought-provoking, with a subtle humour, and unexpected phrasing that makes the ordinary a new experience. They move with assurance in the world of fairy-tale possibilities, tilting the reader's perspective on the ordinary and expected, which is one of the powers of fantasy.

ALTHOUGH COLLECTIONS OF FOLK- and fairy-tales, and picture book retellings, were common in Canada throughout the twentieth century, there were few novels re-imagining such stories until around the turn of the millennium. On the whole, these were well-done fantasies; the magic in *The Snow Queen* and *An Earthly Knight* came with the cores of the stories from their literary fairy-tale and ballad sources and became an organic part of the modern novels. The fantasy in these is an essential and natural element of

---

[2] Palmer, *The Maestro*, p. 47.
[3] *ibid.*, p. 74.
[4] *ibid.*, p. 115.

the original, which is expanded into the novels' deeper range. Palmer's whimsical and fantastical worlds, also built on traditional elements, are harmonious in their whole. The least convincing parts of any of the books discussed in this category are those invented creatures in *After Hamelin*, the Trolavian and the Skipping Dragon, who in their shallow and unintegrated "Whee, this is fantasy so I can do anything" silliness are so at odds with the rest of the story and so hard to accept as real within it.

VI
HISTORICAL FANTASY

HISTORICAL FICTION TELLS a story set in the past; historical fantasy is historical fiction which includes elements of fantasy in the past world. The magic and supernatural beings portrayed in historical fantasy are consistent with the folklore and myths of the setting. One of the most famous is K.M. Briggs' *Hobberdy Dick* (1955), which is set in the aftermath of the English Civil War (the second half of the seventeenth century) and is about the hobgoblin which has looked after a family and manor since time immemorial, who finds himself and all the old folk-customs rejected by the new Puritan owners. Mary Stewart's *Merlin* novels, beginning with *The Crystal Cave* (1970), are another; Dark Age Britain is portrayed with attention to historical accuracy as well as to the traditional "historical" Arthurian matter of Geoffrey of Monmouth, with Merlin not a wizard, but a seer, a prophet, in keeping with the blend of pagan and Christian beliefs probable in post-Roman Britain. Lang's *The Gold of Fairnilee*, discussed above, could also be called historical fantasy. *Shadow in Hawthorn Bay* (1986), Janet Lunn's story of a Scottish immigrant with the second sight, wooed by the ghost of her lover, is one of the few twentieth-century examples of Canadian historical fantasy. A more recent one is McNaughton's *An Earthly Knight* (2002), which, although discussed above as a re-imagining of an older tale (page 76), could equally well be described as historical fantasy; the historical approach lends itself particularly well to re-imaginings of myth, legend, folktales, and ballads.[1]

The Alchemist's Daughter (J/YA)

Eileen Kernaghan's *The Alchemist's Daughter* (2004) is set in England in 1587. A book for young people with an Elizabethan setting will almost inevitably fulfil certain requirements: the hero

---

[1] *The Serpent Bride: Stories From Medieval Danish Ballads* (1998) is a slightly earlier Canadian work which both descriptions also suit.

will meet Shakespeare and save the Queen from assassination—Geoffrey Trease's *Cue For Treason* (1940) casts a long shadow! Kernaghan's book meets these conditions in a manner that is fresh and engaging, while also being well-researched. The hero, Sidonie Quince, is the daughter of a näive and obsessed alchemist. Although the alchemical quest to create gold is presented as a futile undertaking, Sidonie is gifted with the ability to see the future. During the Renaissance, there were believers in both alchemy and prophecy; the author's decision to present one type of mysticism as irrational and another as possible makes for a contrast which would have been shared by many people at the time, who took the Bible as evidence for the possibility of prophecy, but doubted, sometimes as much for religious reasons as for any rational observations of their own, the possibility of man being able to transmute one element to another.

Kernaghan's protagonist greatly distrusts her ability to foresee and prefers to study the rational clarity of mathematics. Fearing that her father, whose experiments are funded by the Queen, will be executed if he fails to create gold, Sidonie and her friend Kit travel to the ruins of Glastonbury Abbey, hoping to find the missing element that will make the transmutation possible. This becomes instead a quest to find the lost treasure of Glastonbury Abbey and to defeat a Catholic conspiracy, in which Sidonie's scrying abilities and the ghost of Sir Philip Sidney play a part. Sidonie also predicts the destruction of Spain's invasion fleet and saves Elizabeth from being poisoned. Spenser, and of course Shakespeare, make brief appearances as well.

Kernaghan writes smooth, well-balanced prose, and presents the details of Elizabethan life and the complexities of alchemy, both its symbolic and its experimental side, with competent ease. Details and explanations are never intruded clumsily, but appear as a natural part of the story. The historical elements are all well researched and Sidonie is a believable and sympathetic protagonist. The weakest element of the story is the conspiracy that dogs Sidonie's quest, which lacks enough presence to make it seem a significant and ongoing danger. The hiding place for the treasure is fairly obvious and, one thinks, among the first places Henry VIII's agents would have looked for missing abbey valuables. The political tensions and the conspiracy are thin compared to the detailed reality of Sidonie's sometimes difficult life with her father, her journey to Glastonbury, or the discussions of alchemy. The story vividly carries readers into Sidonie's life, its sights, sounds, tastes, and anxieties, but it does not quite convince in carrying Sidonie into the heart of political dangers. However, the fantasy elements play an important role in the story and in the characterization of Sidonie, forming a natural and fundamental part of the novel.

Viking Magic series (J)

Australian writer Anna Ciddor's *Runestone* and *Wolfspell*, originally published in Australia in 2002 and 2003 respectively, were republished in Canadian editions in 2004. The decision to bring out these books, little known beyond Australia, for a specifically Canadian market, is indicative of the increasing interest in publishing fantasy within Canada in the years immediately following the turn of the millennium. However, historical fantasy is an area of fantasy in which Canadian authors have to date taken little interest. Although not by a Canadian author, the *Viking Magic* series is noteworthy both because a Canadian publisher evidently felt it had an audience, and because it is written for a younger readership than most Canadian-written fantasy that takes the past as its foundation. It demonstrates that such a novel need not be written for "young adults", as is usually the case in Canada.

Ciddor, in her biography appended to *Wolfspell*, observes that she has based the society in the stories on "real Viking lifestyle and beliefs". She is not writing historical fiction, but depicting an imagined Viking-era world in which folkloric beliefs about Norse magic, as preserved by the later sagas and eddas and deduced (or occasionally invented through the muddling of research and wishful thinking) by nineteenth-century folklorists, are the real magic of the world, and in which many elements of the society are developed from aspects of life in early medieval Scandinavia. The lives of Odda and Thora do brush up against history; in *Wolfspell* there is mention of Norwegian king Harald Fairhair's efforts to unify all Norway under his rule. For the most part, though, the settlement, the wilderness around it, and the distant trading centre and Thing (the assembly of the free men of a district for the settling of disputes, and the place at which they gathered for this) are world enough for the adventures of Thora and Odda. That setting is convincingly rendered and detailed enough to seem another, and very intriguing, world, without overwhelming the reader with a quantity of dry facts.

The story begins in *Runestone* with the births of babies to two neighbouring household. The farmer Bolverk has threatened to throw his child to the wolves if it is female, so the midwife takes the baby girl over the hill, where a family of spellworkers has summoned her to deliver a baby as well. She switches the girl for the spellworkers' boy without anyone knowing, and Oddo is raised as Bolverk the farmer's son, while Thora grows up in the large, exuberant family of spellworkers. There, everything is done by magic; Thora, however, feels more and more useless, since she is incapable of the simplest spells. Oddo, meanwhile, is hopeless at anything to do with tilling and planting, though he can influence the weather and is good with animals. His father continually derides him as useless. When the two meet, Odda gets Thora to reveal her family's spells to him, wanting to work a spell to make his father love him. His effort leaves his father in what is effectively a coma. While waiting for the cure provided by Thora's family to take effect, Thora and Oddo go alone to the distant market to sell Bolverk's goods; Oddo, now more careful in his magical experimentation, uses his new shapeshifting skills to tow their boat. As Oddo's magical abilities improve, he also discovers there is much on the farm he can do because of his affinity with animals, while Thora learns about growing plants and teaches herself to make herbal rather than magical medicines.

In *Wolfspell*, both children continue to develop their new skills and their self-confidence, while struggling to be accepted by their families, neither of which values those skills. Once again they have to work together to protect Oddo's farm, this time from a greedy neighbour, while Oddo's parents have gone to the Thing in Gula to pay the new taxes the king is demanding. Oddo and Thora themselves must journey to the Thing to contest Grimmr the Greedy's claim to Bolverk's land, a journey that puts them in great danger and demands new strength from both of them. Raiding overseas and the slave trade in captives are two aspects of Norse society introduced here; the children are shocked to learn the fate of their friend Ulf's prisoners, but the issue is not presented from any jarringly modern point of view and they make no protests in anachronistic terms. Slavery is an aspect of their society that they had not personally encountered before, though they knew of it. Like Oddo's refusal to kill a wolf while hunting, the reaction to the enslavement of captives is a personal one on the part of the characters; they are not made the mouthpieces of modern *mores*. In this, the book does more towards realistic historical fiction than many "time-travel to learn history" novels ever manage.

In the course of the stories Thora and Odda face great difficulties and dangers, and occasionally come near to losing their lives, but though they are children, not adolescents, the problems and their solutions remain believable in the context of Ciddor's world. Given the magical skills at Oddo's command and Thora's self-reliant common sense, their survival and success against dangerous adult opponents never seems contrived. The world is believable, and Ciddor does an excellent job of presenting it as vast, the children's knowledge of it realistically limited to the local level. Beyond the Gula Thing, the world is all stories to them, an unknown land which hardly ever impinges on their lives. The books are well researched and well written, and very good at providing social and technological detail. The storyline is entertaining, and occasionally thoughtful. The style is not over-simplified, but is not too difficult and the plot moves at a good pace for young readers. The subject matter and the presentation also make these books good candidates for use with young teens possessing poor reading skills. Even though the magic is used for handy things like preventing food poisoning and to make charms against drowning, it nevertheless does not make things too easy. It functions as an integral part of the world Ciddor has created without becoming a mere convenience to give Oddo power.

Unfortunately, the third in Ciddor's trilogy, *Stormriders* (2004) has not come out in a Canadian or American edition and *Runestone* and *Wolfspell* have become difficult to find in North America, as the company which re-issued them appears to have gone out of business. This is a shame, as these books deserve to be read and there is a dearth of good quality, richly-textured novels for the youngest novel readers in any genre, but particularly in fantasy. Too often, young beginning readers are led by the selection available to them in school libraries to dismiss reading as boring, because all that is available is formulaic sports or girls-and-friends or "realistic" school stories in stilted prose. School libraries need more imaginative literature for readers newly embarked upon novels, and series like Nix's *The Seventh Tower* are few and far between. Ciddor's *Viking Magic* should have been a welcome addition to the selection. Fortunate readers will be able to get the first two stories, each of which does stand on its own and can be read independent of the others, from their public library or a used bookstore; more fortunate still are those who may be able to finish their reading of the trilogy courtesy of an Australian friend or relation.

LITTLE HISTORICAL FANTASY HAS BEEN written or published in Canada until recently. Of course, the overlap between what is here called historical fantasy and the re-imagining of traditional or old and familiar stories in modern novel or short story form is large. Historical fantasy lends itself to the retelling of old tales; traditional material, re-imagined and fleshed out into a novel, assumes most naturally an historical setting contemporary with the source. Even so, at the start of the twenty-first century, historical fantasy forms only a small part of Canadian fantasy literature, though what has been written is of very good quality.

VII
ANIMAL FANTASY

THE TERM "ANIMAL FANTASY" has a variety of meanings. Stories about otherwise realistic animals with language and thought of human complexity, such as Richard Adams' *Watership Down* (1972) and satirical political allegory like George Orwell's *Animal Farm* (1945) are both sometimes called animal fantasy. Stories in which the fantastic element is primarily that the animal characters act like humans, as in Kenneth Grahame's *The Wind in the Willows* (1908) or Beatrix Potter's *The Tale of Peter Rabbit* (1901) are also animal fantasy. The many folktales from around the world which feature heroes who are animals (rather than the more obviously fantastic enchanted humans in animal form) are also a type of animal fantasy. A narrower definition limits the term to stories that contain other elements of fantasy, that is, invented cultures and worlds, stories of heroic quests, magic, and the like. One of the few twentieth-century Canadian attempts at this sort of animal fantasy was Margaret Laurence's *Jason's Quest* (1970), the story of a British mole who sets out on a journey to London to discover the cause of his society's stagnation, but the shallow world-building and formulaic plot do not compare well with British examples of the genre. Much earlier, Walter de la Mare had demonstrated the possibilities of animal fantasy in *The Three Mulla-Mulgars* (1910), in which three monkey brothers set off on a quest for their father's homeland, travelling through an Africa inhabited by many strange animal clans and magical beings. A much, much earlier example of a monkey on an heroic quest is the Chinese Buddhist epic *Journey to the West* (c. 1570). This story of a troublesome, trickster monkey leading a monk, a pig, and a dragon transformed to a horse on a quest for Buddhist sutras was composed in its present form in the fifteen-seventies, based on earlier tales both oral and written. It was retold by Evelyn Nagai-Bertrong and Anker Odum as a graphic novel for children, *Adventures of the Magic*

Monkey Along the Silk Road (ROM 1983), to accompany an exhibition at the Royal Ontario Museum called "Silk Roads—China Ships". The format allows aspects of the culture to be explained or illustrated in an entertaining way and the selected episodes of the story hold together very well, making this version entertaining in its own right as well as a good introduction to the source. More recent and better known animal fantasies are British author Brian Jacques' *Redwall* (1986) and the numerous other volumes in the series about Redwall Abbey and the mice and other creatures who defend it against invading tyrants. In the tradition of the best secondary world fantasy, Jacques has created a world of many lands and cultures and a long history.

Firewing (J)

Kenneth Oppel had written several children's speculative fiction novels and humorous fantasies for young children before he made his reputation with *Silverwing* (1997) and *Sunwing* (1999). *Silverwing* won the Canadian Library Association Book of the Year for Children Award in 1998; *Sunwing* in 2000. These are animal fantasies that follow the pattern of traditional quests, except that the main characters are young bats, Shade and Marina. An ancient war between owls and bats, religious differences, a new war begun by murder, human evil, and a psychopathic villain are the main components of the series.

The cosmology of Oppel's bat world becomes central to the story in *Firewing* (2002), the third in the series. Griffin, the child of Shade and Marina, is pulled into the Underworld through a crack in the earth. Shade sets out to save his son, while Griffin joins Luna and other dead bats, discovering that even what appears to be the afterlife is filled with danger and uncertainty as to which beliefs about life, death, and the gods are true. Griffin confronts past sins and is hunted by Goth, his father's enemy. Goth is still, despite his death, the servant of Cama Zotz, the god who wants to destroy all life and rule a world of the dead. Shade's confrontation with Zotz at the book's conclusion and the sacrifice demanded of him make for a powerful conclusion.

Even in *Silverwing*, the cosmology of the world, the relationship between the bats and their goddess Nocturna and the ancient conflict between the deities, plays an important role; as the series progresses this comes more and more to shape the plot, until in *Firewing* it dominates the story. Oppel is consistent throughout the series in his portrayal of the bats' world, continuing to develop ideas introduced in *Silverwing*. The enduring sound-pictures which record bat history in *Silverwing* have by *Firewing* developed into apparently solid worlds created by Zotz from sound alone. The development of Shade as an epic hero through the three books is also a significant fantasy element. He grows from a brash, foolhardy youngster to a wise and rightfully self-assured adult, capable of undertaking a perilous quest not on impulse or to prove himself, but out of sober and grim necessity.

Feather and Bone: The Crow Chronicles (J/YA)

The Mob (2004) is the first in Clem Martini's trilogy *Feather and Bone: The Crow Chronicles*. Martini, a playwright who usually writes about troubled teens, sets a society of crows in western Canada, with a complex culture of laws, traditions, and mythology shaping their lives. The first book is narrated by Kalum, an older crow who is the Chooser, the arbitrator and guardian of the flock's traditions. The hero is Kyp, a reckless young crow who is temporarily banished to reflect on a serious error of judgement. During a spring blizzard Kyp and his friend Kym, a dedicated human-watcher, both break taboos as they independently lead groups to shelter in forbidden places.

The Mob presents a well-developed crow society, with many details of real crow behaviour as well as the imagined aspects of higher crow culture; the two elements fuse smoothly and convincingly. Although Kyp is the one who precipitates the action and resolves the crisis, it is the narrator, Kalum, who displays the strongest personality; his reflective, self-critical, "old-mannish" manner does tend to slow the narrative down in some places. The style of narration and the simplicity of the story at times seem aimed at different audiences or reading levels. Weak readers may find Kalum's narrative style somewhat slow going. In contrast, the events of the story are very simple and straightforward—too much so for the more able reader expecting a greater degree of plot and character complexity in a tale into which so much world-building energy has gone. Much of the interest is generated by the unfolding of the details of crow society, and their (particularly Kym's) perspectives on human behaviour.

However, the second book in the series, *The Plague* (2005) is a more even, mature work than its predecessor. The plot is more complex, more in tune with the literary style and the complexity of the background. The new narrator, Katakata, although still a character who is able credibly to comment on and explain crow culture to his uninitiated listeners within the story (and thus to the readers), is an exiled crow from another family who joins Kyp and the few survivors of a human-induced crow plague in a continent-spanning journey to rescue Kym from a research facility. Even more so than in the first book, the world and culture of Martini's crows is richly detailed and always believable. Realistic crow behaviour again provides the foundation for all aspects of the society, while the fantasy element, the sentience of the crows and their long oral history and mythology, is handled with consistency throughout. The trilogy concludes with *The Judgment* (2006).

DESPITE THE EXISTENCE of such classics as *The Wind in the Willows* and *The Three Mulla-Mulgars* to serve as examples of the range of possibilities, or the evident desire for good animal fantasy demonstrated by the enormous and enduring popularity of *Redwall* and Jacques' many other connected titles, little of it has been written in Canada. In the United States, books such as Katherine Lasky's continuing *Guardians of Ga'Hoole* series (2003) show the influence not only of Jacques, but of Oppel's bat fantasies, the popularity of which is not confined to Canada. Oppel and Martini demonstrate a great advancement in Canadian animal fantasy since the cardboard world of Laurence's moles; Oppel's bats and Martini's crows exist in fully-realized fantasy worlds and are novels capable, as Oppel has demonstrated, of holding their own internationally.

VIII
DUAL-WORLD FANTASY

DUAL-WORLD FANTASY IS REALLY only a type of secondary world fantasy in which the secondary world (the invented world) is in some way connected to the primary world, our real world. Good stories of this type present alternate or secondary worlds that are just as carefully created and as thoroughly realized as pure secondary world fantasies, but, as in Lewis' *Chronicles of Narnia*, the characters start off in our world and pass into another by magic. As in Lewis, elements of the secondary world may also cross over to enter the primary world, our own real world; the story is in part about the contacts between the two and the experiences of the characters who move from one to the unfamiliar other. Just as with secondary world fantasy in which the imagined world has no contact or connection with ours and is the only world existing for the purposes of the story, the alternate worlds entered by characters from the primary world may explore other social or cultural possibilities, or be used to exaggerate some facet of the real world to emphasize some point, or may be intended in part to offer a contrast and suggest alternatives to some aspect of our own culture.

Lewis's *The Lion, The Witch and the Wardrobe* (1950) and the six other *Narnia* books are the most famous example of this type of fantasy. L. Frank Baum's *The Wonderful Wizard of Oz* (1900) and its sequels are really another; even though Oz is supposed to be located somewhere on our own Earth and could be reached over desert and by sea, it had its own rules of reality and magic and little connection to the primary world save for the people and animals who occasionally found their way from it into Oz. Michael Ende's *The Neverending Story* (1979/1983) is another classic dual-world fantasy. The multiple worlds of many of Diana Wynne Jones's books, such as *Charmed Life* (1977), *The Homeward Bounders* (1981), *Howl's Moving Castle* (1986), and *The*

Merlin Conspiracy (2003), are further examples of stories set in magical worlds which can be reached from our own, although our world is likely to be only one of many realities the heroes encounter, a strange and disturbing place seen through new eyes. Garth Nix, who has already earned a place as one of the best fantasists of the twenty-first century, has begun a seven-book series, *The Keys to the Kingdom* (2003-), which commences in the near future of our world and follows the hero into the House of the Architect, the epicentre of creation. In a reversal of perspective, within the vast world of the House all worlds inhabited by mortals—planets across space and time in the universe rather than multiple realities—are referred to as "Secondary Realms".

In the twentieth century, few examples of dual-world fantasy in Canada were written. Ruth Nichols' *A Walk Out of the World* (1969) and *The Marrow of the World* (1972) are almost the only examples before the end of the century, and although well-received by critics at the time, they do not compare favourably with contemporary children's fantasy in Britain and the United States; the apparent novelty of their fantasy setting (actually fairly shallow and generic even for the time) seems to have led to the overlooking of weak plots and characterization.

The contrast between the primary and secondary worlds in dual-world fantasy can be used as part of the story, a means of freeing young heroes from the constraints of their society, giving them the opportunity to confront greater and more dramatic challenges than they might in their ordinary lives. Through this, it can provide a metaphoric means of dramatizing struggles that everyone goes through on the way to maturity. It can also be used as a means of exploring and explaining an alternate society, by providing a protagonist to whom the world is as new and unfamiliar as it is to the reader; reader and hero discover the world together. Unfortunately, it can also be used as a shortcut to throw a character into a world of stock fantasy elements, an "excuse" for shoddily constructed unreality to make the fantasy "easy" and palatable for those who do not want to expend effort in understanding a new world. Such use reduces the fantasy to the level of a condescending "Let's pretend ...", a wink to say we all know we do not have to take it seriously, because it is not as real as the real world. At its best, though, dual-world fantasy is taken just as seriously by its creators as the best secondary world fantasy, of which it is a subset, and offers its readers a new world in which to immerse themselves.

The *Unicorn* series (J)

Vicki Blum's unicorn series began with *Wish Upon a Unicorn* (1999), which, although her third children's book, was her first fantasy. This was followed by *The Shadow Unicorn* (2000), *The Land Without Unicorns* (2001), *The Promise of the Unicorn* (2002) and *A Gathering of Unicorns* (2003). The story begins with Arica, a modern Canadian girl, who falls through a crack in her grandmother's kitchen floor (which is very difficult to picture as described) and immediately encounters two trolls in the cellar below. She follows them through a tunnel into another world, is captured, and put in a labour camp with elves and unicorns. The land is divided into North Bundelag and South Bundelag. The North, ruled by a Fairy Queen, is inhabited by elves, fairies, and unicorns, the South by humans. The villain of the series is Raden, eldest son of the Fairy Queen. Raden is growing rich through slave labour, mining for the metal-greedy South. In the first book, Arica frees Wish, the baby unicorn, discovers she can communicate telepathically with unicorns, escapes, and is sent home by the Fairy Queen, who turns out to be her grandmother. Her parents are conveniently made to forget she ever vanished.

In the subsequent books Arica returns, sometimes with her cousin Connor. *The Shadow Unicorn* sees her trying to break a spell that has turned all the unicorns to stone; she discovers that she and her grandmother are the only fairies left, all the others having vanished. They may, like her father, have lost their memories and be living new lives in our world. She fights a duel with a unicorn allied with Raden, using a magic sword that is in charge of the battle, a fight that is not convincing given the difference in size, strength, and skill of the two combatants, convenient magic sword or not. In *The Land Without Unicorns,* Arica and Connor are sent by the Fairy Queen to South Bundelag to retrieve a magic book that lists all the living fairies; she uses Wish's magic to call the missing fairies home. In the final two volumes, she has to find a magic flower to save her mother, who has been poisoned by Raden, and resolve a war between North and South Bundelag.

The books are simply written and suitable for beginning novel readers. They would also be suitable for older children with reading problems, since they feature a simple prose style and diction, and simple ideas, with plenty of story and vivid physical descriptions. However, the covers (unicorns over-endowed with eyelashes, framed, on the first, with lush roses), are almost guaranteed to put boys off, though the stories themselves would otherwise appeal equally to girls and boys. Characterization is limited to one or two descriptive traits. The plots, particularly in the first book, rely heavily on coincidence. The world Arica enters is never convincing as a real world. The political background figures strongly as the motivating factor in the plots, most of which are driven by Raden's rebellion against his mother, yet one never has the impression of a real, functioning kingdom. The Fairy Queen does nothing about the enslavement of her people in the first book and seems hardly aware of it, nor has she taken any action against Raden. It is pure chance that Arica stumbles into the situation and precipitates an end to it. The magic is a convenience, a means of allowing Arica, using some item or power gained by chance, to suddenly defeat enemies much larger and stronger than herself.

Although the world and its magic are never developed in any depth, they are likely to be exciting and novel to the youngest "chapter book" readers who have not been exposed to any more demanding fantasy literature, though those more widely read are likely to find them thin. However, though shallow and frequently over-convenient, the world does have internal consistency; it sticks to its own rules, which is an important factor in creating a believable fantasy. The books tell coherent and internally consistent stories. For what the series is, it works well: an enjoyable, if undemanding and coincidence-prone, tale. With the current declining reading levels in Canada, there is a need for imaginative stories suitable for children who cannot read what their peers even a few decades ago were reading when they began novels, but who want a story to take them away from the here and now; Blum's books form part of a small body of recent works meeting that need, in which the fantasy is not mere window-dressing.

The Mermaid Secret (J)

Blum followed her *Unicorn* series with a book written to the same formula: young female heroes who suddenly discover that their father was not human and was from another world, which only they can save. This one features mermaids. *The Mermaid Secret* (2004) is about twins, practical Danya, the narrator, and dreamer Kallie. The mermaid Brin comes to Kallie in human form to tell her that the twins are special and the mermaids need their help. Kallie drags Danya to Aryalon, the mermaids' ocean world, with a spell. There they discover that they were born in Aryalon to a human mother and a merman father. In Aryalon, they grow mermaid tails and can breathe underwater. They return to earth to retrieve a magic jewel stolen by a scuba diver, but when the jewel is destroyed, they need to find another means to keep the magic from draining out of Aryalon. This is simply accomplished through an undramatic visit to the sea nymphs in the deep ocean, who restore the fragmented jewel.

As in the *Unicorn* series, characters, plot, and world are simple, and the fantasy element is superficially conceived, although internally consistent and integral to the story. The mermaids live in a "mercity" and cook on "merfire" which burns underwater. It is an idealistic world without money, where everything is shared because there is plenty, but how this works in practice, like the convenient, foundationless and problem-free magic, is never explored. The twins never develop beyond the initial traits used to distinguish them. Like the *Unicorn* series as well, *The Mermaid Secret* makes a useful "beginning chapter book", quickly outgrown, but has little in it to appeal to fantasy readers who want enduring depth and thought in their stories. Like the *Unicorn* series, it works for what it is.

The Watcher's Quest trilogy (YA)

Margaret Buffie has written a number of novels for teens, most of which feature misfits, eccentrics, and the paranormal. Buffie's *The Watcher* (2000), the first in a trilogy, starts off as though it is to be a coming of age story about a misfit teen in an eccentric but loving family. Gradually, it becomes apparent that there is another world, one to which the main character discovers both she and her sister belong. Although Buffie's world is not that of the Irish myths, she utilises its character names and relationships, as well as the passionate, self-absorbed emotions of the Irish gods and heroes, for her inhuman, otherworldly characters. The heroic ethos which sometimes seems to view conflict as the noblest of pastimes is also transferred from the world of Irish epic to this new world.

Buffie's hero, Emma, learns that both she and her sister belong to another world. Emma herself is a Watcher, who must guard the girl she has believed to be her younger sister, Summer. Summer is a changeling, rightful queen of an island kingdom but also hostage and pawn in a game being played between powerful and capricious beings. The two worlds are not completely separate; Emma and Summer do not suddenly find themselves transported to another realm for convenient adventure. Characters cross back and forth, just as mysterious and threatening in our world as in the one from which Emma originally came. The lives of ordinary humans, completely unaware of the other world and innocent of its conflicts, are threatened and disrupted. As in the case of traditional fairy changelings, the real child of Emma's parents has been taken, so not only does she have Summer to protect and her own ambiguous place in the other world to come to terms with, but she feels she must rescue the unknown human daughter and return her to her rightful family. The book follows contemporary trends in "literary" writing in being entirely in the present tense, which can become irritating and distracting, rather than conveying the immediacy the style is probably meant to evoke. However, the characters are well-developed and the other world feels as solid as Emma's Saskatchewan. The novel's sequels, *The Seeker* (2002) and *The Finder* (2004), continue to develop the complex plot and the character relationships, as Emma struggles to survive the game in which she has found herself while asserting her independence of it and restoring her suffering human family. She moves from being a servant and a piece in the game to a player taking control, and discovers her true father has been behind much of the action, using her and the games themselves in an effort to end such games, which destroy not only individual lives, but whole societies. The worlds of the story continue to develop with internal consistency, and in imaginative complexity, integral to the plot, making this trilogy a well-executed fantasy.

The Wolves of Woden (J/YA)

Alison Baird's *The Wolves of Woden* (2001) is a "prequel" to *The Hidden World* (1999), but seems a much more powerful and confident story than its predecessor, showing the mature style Baird would shortly after bring to her *Willowmere Chronicles* (see above, page 50). In *Wolves*, sixteen year-old Jean MacDougall plays a leading role in events in the parallel world of Annwn, and the reader feels that the kingdoms and people there exist for their own sake, rather than for the convenience of a hero in need of an adventure in order to cope with the stress of real life, as is the case in parts of *The Hidden World*, which is about Jean's granddaughter.

Jean's story begins in Newfoundland in the summer of 1940. She feels impotent in the face of war but has what the Scots call second sight, which connects her with the fairy otherworld. Jean passes into the world of Annwn, to the fairies' Isle of Avalon. This occupies the geographical position of the Avalon peninsula in Newfoundland. Annwn is between the world of divine light and Jean's world, the Shadow World. There she meets humans, settlers who came long ago from Ireland and Wales, and is swept into their war against the invading Lochlannach, descendants of Vikings. Following Irish tradition, the fairies of this book are the angels who refused to choose between God and the rebel angels and were cast out, not to hell, but to earth.

The war is not merely between humans; it is being pushed on by the god Woden, who wants to bring about the end of the worlds. To counter this, High King Diarmait, Queen Gwenlian, and the druid Lailoken want to find the Spear of Lugh, from Irish mythology, which in this story is identified with the Spear of Longinus from medieval Christian legend. Jean becomes central to this search, passing back and forth between the worlds, in both of which her friends are risking their lives in battle.

Jean is a well-developed and believable character, although some of the other important figures, such as Gwenlian and her husband, are mere conventional sketches. One of the most interesting characters is Morgana, an ambiguous and ultimately treacherous ally, born of a human father and a fairy mother, at home among neither people. One of the most frequent flaws in fantasy, even on the part of those who have not cynically set out to assemble a generic world and plot from stock parts, is the villain whose evil is a descriptor, like eye-colour, without any complexity in motivation, character, or desires. Baird avoids this. Her depiction of Morgana makes her convincingly real; to use the analogy of the angels, she is a person in the process of falling.

The blending of Celtic and Norse mythology, Arthurian legend, and fairy lore is deftly handled, and the conflicts external and internal satisfying and credible. *The Wolves of Woden* is an all-round strong fantasy.

The Serpent's Egg trilogy (J)

The first books by J. Fitzgerald McCurdy (for her later work, see above, page 64) were *The Serpent's Egg* (2001), *The Burning Crown* (2002), and *The Twisted Blade* (2003). The story follows the adventures of Miranda, a Canadian girl who enters another world through a "portal" under Parliament Hill. There, she discovers she is supposed to be a key player in a war between Elves and an imprisoned demon called Hate. In all, Miranda makes three trips to the other world. In *The Serpent's Egg*, Hate escapes her prison, enters our world, and pursues Miranda. Miranda's mother mysteriously vanishes and Miranda, without appearing particularly worried by this, goes to the other world with a stranger who shows up at her house, the druid Naim. In the other world, after a number of formulaic encounters, Miranda eventually finds the Serpent's Egg and seals Hate into her prison. *The Burning Crown* sees Miranda and her friends trying to retrieve the elven crown from Hate's servants. In *The Twisted Blade*, Hate has freed the skeletal King of the Dead, who makes war on Elves and Dwarves using hordes of the dead. Miranda must help find the Twisted Blade which can destroy Hate.

The prose style is juvenile; the books read as though they were written by an enthusiastic fourteen-year-old, dripping with exclamation marks, words all in uppercase any time anyone raises a voice, bizarrely incongruous similes, and redundancies. Examples from *The Twisted Blade* illustrate this: "A terrible loneliness came over him. He felt as if he were alone in an empty universe...";[1] and "Instead of driving him [Otovite] mad, the King's lethal laughter made Otavite so mad...".[2] In a world free of any evidence of industrialisation or, for that matter, any evidence of trade or agriculture to support the society of nobles and soldiers, both rubber raincoats and hubcaps are used as similes. "Otavite watched, horrified, as the leathery hide seemed to fold into itself before crumpling to the floor like a rubberized raincoat. The Giant's eyes, round as hubcaps...".[3] There is no external narrator whose voice is apparent, to whom such "external" similes could be attributed, as there is for the "whistle of an engine coming out of a tunnel"[4] of the narration of *The Hobbit*. Thus, the rubber raincoat and the hubcap are intimately linked with the context of the limited third person narration following the giant Otovite. If the same similes had been used in a passage where the narration was following Miranda, they would not have been so jarring. Further muddled thinking is displayed when the aftermath of an astroid's impact on Earth millions of years ago is described as a "nuclear holocaust",[5] despite there being nothing nuclear about it.

Characters fail to act consistently or realistically. Hate describes Miranda as "a wicked human child"[6] and two pages later "the wicked Elf child".[7] (Her parents are only later revealed to be Elves.) In the same book a soldier, creeping through a fort filled with the bodies of his dead comrades, decides that it is too dangerous to make a light because enemies might notice him, and yet he talks aloud to himself the whole time. The mysterious disappearance of Miranda's mother at the start of *The Serpent's Egg* is eventually explained, three books later: she claims she suddenly went to Disneyland to allow her daughter to undertake the adventure, an explanation that makes little sense within the story and further undermines any literary belief one might hope to develop in the characters.

Character is always labelled—good, evil, noble, etc.— rather

---

[1] McCurdy, *The Twisted Blade*, pp. 5-6.
[2] ibid. p. 19.
[3] ibid. p. 15.
[4] Tolkien, *The Hobbit*, 4th Edn. p. 23.
[5] McCurdy, *The Serpent's Egg*, p. 86.
[6] McCurdy, *The Twisted Blade*, p. 19.
[7] ibid. p. 21.

than being revealed or even backed up by actions. Readers are meant to accept these designations as instructed. In the first book we are told repeatedly that Penelope is annoying and in the later two that she has changed to become a friend, but the stories show no development or change in any character, even the hero, Miranda. In the conclusion of the final book, Nicholas's parents are very blasé when told that their son, missing in our world since an earthquake caused by Hate, is staying for the summer in another world of which they have not heard until that very moment. Nicholas seems to feel no compunction about doing so, no need to justify his choice to his parents or even to let them know he is alive. None of the characters react convincingly to the dramatic events in which they are involved; they overreact at odd times, running from the room in hysterics when given a fairly prosaic piece of information, but displaying very brief grief and returning to bratty banter a moment after witnessing someone they know well apparently die. None of the characters evolve; they appear unchanged by experience, by suffering and loss or fear of loss or consequences, unaffected by encountering a wider world.

The role of the child heroes in events never seems essential in *The Serpent's Egg* trilogy. Although one of Miranda's friends precipitates the search for the weapon that can destroy Hate, one cannot believe in a ruler and court who regard as a brilliant inspiration a child's suggestion that they send messengers out to ask if anyone knows where to find the missing Twisted Blade. Miranda's failure to act against Hate at the end, even though she knows Hate has killed thousands and will kill thousands or millions more in two worlds, is because she believes killing Hate will mean she is just as evil as the demon. Whatever one may think of Miranda's ethics, her pacifism is undermined (though never questioned) a moment later, once others have conveniently dealt with the villains for her, when she crushes the demon's last egg without compunction. Killing an infant demon which has thus far committed no wrong is apparently less heinous than killing a genocidal tyrant who plans the annihilation of all life and is about to kill you. The contrast with Taran, who spares the fledgling Gwythaint, servant of evil Arawn, in Lloyd Alexander's *The Book of Three*, is marked.

The appeal of the series to some readers lies in its superficial appearance of inventiveness. Although shallow and largely limited to genre stereotypes (noble elves, brusque and testy dwarves) or one-off jokes that serve no function and strain literary belief (giantpecker birds which exist only to peck on giants' heads and provide backchat), this will seem quite novel for many young readers not yet widely read. It contains elements that those with a very limited exposure to fantasy will not have previously encountered: a wide world with a range of magical peoples and a history that shapes the present action. Though the plot has the appearance of complexity, in that it is long and has many episodes, with a narrative that follows several different characters, it is all very predictable. It is simplistic in interconnections of cause and effect, lacking any subtlety. Although the series seems to aspire to heroic scope and grandeur, the story and the style lack any elevation in thought or feeling; there is no range of style or emotion. Everyone—elves, dwarves, modern children, giants—thinks and acts more or less the same way, although the non-humans are not quite as goofy and childish as the humans. None of those presented as characters for the young heroes to admire and learn from are shown to be any wiser or nobler than the children themselves; there is nothing to aspire to, no different mode of being. As Miranda enters her parents' world and allegedly grows into her destined role as its saviour—a role that never seems to fit her— her part in the action remains contrived and is never convincingly essential.

The Serpent's Egg trilogy aspires to be a story of epic heroism and the salvation of a world, but in the end, it succeeds only in being the sort of imitative story that is written by enthusiastic children themselves. Children with limited reading experience (in part due to so much good literature of past decades being removed from schools and libraries because even the authors of the nineteen-sixties and -seventies are "old" and "hard"), have not been exposed to much good writing or good fantasy, and cannot tell the difference between good and poor writing, or between clichéed superficiality and well-integrated use of traditional elements or new invention. The novelty and excitement of such bad fantasy engages them, for a time, but in the long run poor writing sours them on fantasy, as they come to view the genre itself as trite and predicable.

Jayden's Rescue (J)

Jayden's Rescue (2002) endeavours to be instruction disguised as "fun", in the tradition of Norton Juster's *The Phantom Tollbooth* (1961). Vladimir Tumanov's aim in this, his only book, seems to be to encourage the reader's interest in mathematics. The three heroes, Alex, Vanessa, and Sam, must solve a series of math problems found in a magical book that appears without any explanation on Alex's bookshelf. In the story within that book, the imprisoned Queen Jayden must solve four hundred problems in order to escape a sorcerer's dungeon through a series of locked, guarded rooms. To discover what happens next, the children must solve each problem; Jayden magically receives their solutions and is able to move to the next room in the sequence. To avoid the sorcerer's vengeance once she is free, the children must complete more problems. In the real world, Alex is nearly killed when the sorcerer cuts the tow rope while he is water-skiing.

The premise of this book is logically flawed; ironic in a work so concerned with the logic of mathematical word-problems. If Jayden is real, as she must be if the sorcerer is real and can cut a rope in Alex's world, then, since we are told that Jayden is an excellent mathematician and a highly-regarded teacher, there should be no need for children in another world to solve her math problems. If the story Alex is reading is only a magical means of making him work at his math problems—that is, if it is not "real" in relation to Alex's reality but is only an illusion, dream, or magical lesson—then the penalty for failure cannot be real death. No explanation for the magical book is ever offered, or for Jayden the adult mathematician's need to have children solve her math problems. The characters are mere outlines. No effort is made to make a story that is internally consistent or that holds together logically. The fantasy is a thin excuse to demonstrate the correct method of working through mathematical word problems, and nothing more.

Cat's Eye Corner and The Silver Door (J)

Terry Griggs' *Cat's Eye Corner* (2002) and *The Silver Door* (2004) are also books similar to Juster's *The Phantom Tollbooth* (1961) in being humorous stories devoted to wordplay. Juster's book is intended to promote an interest in learning, however, while those of Griggs, whose other works are adult non-fantasy fiction, have humour as the primary purpose.

In the first story, Olivier is sent on a scavenger hunt around a bizarre house by his step-grandmother. He encounters a number of odd characters, who provide him with the objects he seeks and help him prevent a villain from rewriting the dictionary. In the second, Olivier enters a world ruled by the child-hating Emperor of Ice Cream in pursuit of his kidnapped friend, the magical fountain pen Murray Shaeffer. He encounters Spelling Bees, a shop that sells literal Turncoats, Life Jackets, Smoking Jackets, and Dust Jackets, and a girl named Sharon who ferries them over the river Stynx. The story makes much use of such embodied puns, not all of which (like the aside that Murray Shaeffer sometimes writes music) will be perceived right away by many younger readers, though that is no reason not to include them.

Though the Emperor and his ice cream, which extends life but induces selfishness and a hatred of children, are defeated with the help of a magical remote control, the plot and its ultimate resolution are weak. The Emperor's world never loses the feel of something made up as a vehicle for the puns. Its restoration, which happens "off-stage" with the freeing of the child-slaves by their parents, lacks any dramatic impact. The doubles of the Emperor and his wife who have invaded Cat's Eye Corner are simply a device to put the remote in Olivier's hands and to have Murray stolen. Their disappearance at the end is a yet another convenience, lacking drama or any effort on Olivier's part. The characters undergo little to test or change them; they exist to function as puns. The fantasy element in the story is essential to it, but like the characters and the plot, exists to provide an excuse for the wordplay and, again like character and plot, is subservient to that wordplay. There is nothing capable of engendering literary belief in the reader. Many parts of the story are very briefly funny, but as a whole, the book lacks coherency and dramatic integrity.

DUAL-WORLD FANTASY WAS UNCOMMON in Canadian children's literature in the twentieth century. Although there was a significant increase in such books around the turn of the millennium, improvement in the literary quality of the fantasy since the days of Nichols' *A Walk Out of the World* has been uneven. Buffie and

Baird develop their secondary worlds with care and attention to the creation of an internally-cohesive and rich reality. Their dual-world stories are good literature and good fantasy. Blum's worlds, although shallow, are internally consistent, while the stories she writes are workmanlike and, again, internally consistent; though there is little depth to characters or plots the stories are engaging and are a good stepping stone for imaginative beginning readers on their way to richer fantasy worlds. However, dual-world fantasy has been used by others as an excuse for flinging primary world child-heroes into worlds assembled from stock parts, characterized by slapdash invention and slipshod and illogical plotting, where the pervasive attitude that "fantasy doesn't have to make sense" allows poor-quality literature into print. This ultimately runs the risk of putting readers off fantasy altogether, by leading to the dismissal of the whole corpus of fantasy literature as clichéed, self-contradictory, and poorly-crafted. Dual-world fantasy itself is not the cause of this—one of the best and most important children's fantasists of the second half of the twentieth century, Diana Wynne Jones, writes primarily dual or multiple-world fantasy—but its combination of a secondary world with a primary world narrative perspective to act as "tour-guide" perhaps means that dual-world fantasy is simpler to abuse in this way than pure secondary world fantasy.

Writing dual-world fantasy looks easy to those who take a sudden notion that fantasy is popular and they should write one too; the difficulty of doing it well proves that it is not.

IX
SECONDARY AND ALTERNATE WORLD FANTASY

SECONDARY WORLD FANTASY IS fantasy set in a created world. The definition of "sub-creation" in the second edition of the *Oxford English Dictionary* (1989) is "J. R. R. Tolkien's word for the process of inventing an imaginary or secondary world, different from the primary world but internally consistent." This also contains a definition of secondary world fantasy: fantasy literature set in such an imaginary world, "different from the primary world but internally consistent". There is a subtle difference between secondary worlds that are entirely different from our own and alternate worlds that are "what if" versions of the primary world. Sometimes such alternate worlds are founded on a change in history; "alternate history" is a thriving branch of adult fantasy, with such authors as Harry Turtledove specialising in it. Although less common in writing for children, alternate histories are part of the background of Diana Wynne Jones' concept of "related worlds" underlying the Chrestomanci series: what if Guy Fawkes had succeeded in blowing up Parliament? What if Napoleon had won at Waterloo? These are not usually the pressing issues or even the obvious differences in Jones' worlds, but they underlie the shape the twentieth century has taken in some of her alternate worlds. Sometimes alternate worlds are "what ifs" of the laws of nature: what if magic existed? Many of Jones' worlds are like this. Patricia C. Wrede's *Mairelon the Magician* (1991) and *The Magician's Ward* (1997), and, co-written with Caroline Stevermer, *Sorcery and Cecelia* (1988), are set in a world like our own, with the addition of magic, which is constrained by its own natural laws and by rules, rituals, and traditions on the part of its practitioners. The subtle differences in an England which has a Royal College of Wizards and Ministry of Wizardry, combined with the familiar, open up new possibilities for the imagination to explore. Joan Aiken's *Wolves Chronicles* (1962-2005) are set in a world where the Stuarts never lost the throne of the United Kingdom and Hanoverian pretenders are a constant terrorist threat to the crown.

Most often, the term "secondary world" is used when the world is clearly not our own. The other worlds to which the protagonists go in stories such as Lewis' *The Lion, the Witch and the Wardrobe* (1950) or in the various series by Vicki Blum discussed above as dual-world fantasy (pages 90-92) are secondary worlds, as is, for practical purposes, Baum's Oz, having not only its own history, geography, and cultures, but its own laws of nature and magic. The many connected worlds of Jones' books are vast groupings of secondary worlds among which the primary world is only a minor subset of reality. Most often, though, a secondary world exists entirely independently, whole and entire. Tolkien's Middle-earth was not conceived by him as a separate invented world, but as an imagined time of our own, yet it is a secondary world in no way identifiable with our own reality from any internal evidence. The nameless little kingdom of MacDonald's *The Princess and the Goblin* (1872), Lloyd Alexander's Prydain (*The Book of Three* 1964) and Westmark (1981), Tove Jansson's Moominvalley (*Comet in Moominland* 1946/1951), Pratchett's Discworld (*The Colour of Magic* 1983; *The Wee Free Men* 2003), Jones' Dalemark (*Cart and Cwidder* 1975), McKinley's Damar and Homeland (*The Blue Sword* 1982), Nix's Old Kingdom (*Sabriel* 1995) and Dark World (*The Seventh Tower: The Fall* 2000) all exist without any reference to or necessary existence of our own world within their reality.[1]

In the adult genre, secondary world fantasy is perhaps the most common. In children's books it does not seem to dominate to the same extent, possibly in part due to the difficulty of creating a believable world with a complex, detailed history and culture within the shorter length of most children's books. However, even in *The Hobbit* (1937), written for children before *The Lord of the Rings* was ever thought of, the world in which Bilbo Baggins goes adventuring is much larger than the story told, its geography and history stretching off the canvas into the far distances of the "leg-

---

[1] The Discworld, which began in satire and expanded into literature beyond any definition, does occasionally bump up against the primary world these days, as the Roundworld invented by the wizards (*The Science of Discworld* 1999). But nobody on Discworld particularly cares.

endarium" on which Tolkien had by then been working for much of his adult life. That a secondary world can be made rich, complex, and original even in a very short format is ably demonstrated by Garth Nix's *The Seventh Tower* series, which is aimed at early novel readers.

When it comes to Canadian children's literature, however, secondary world fantasy was simply absent through most of the twentieth century. Although secondary worlds were created, they were always connected to the primary world, as in the two novels by Ruth Nichols discussed as dual-world fantasy. Only at the very end of the twentieth century did Canadian publishers tentatively bring out a few pure secondary world fantasies, by writers such as Linda Smith, Karleen Bradford, and Martine Bates (Martine Leavitt), all discussed below, as well as Sean Stewart.[2] His novel *Nobody's Son* (1993) tells the story of a hero who wins the hand of a princess, but in doing so unleashes ancient evil on the land; the main story is of the young couple's adventures dealing with this after their marriage. Stewart's novel, which returns to traditions not unknown in some of the more obscure fairy-tales and medieval Romances in having the young husband and wife questing together, is set in a fully-realized secondary world built on the foundation of fairy-tale and Romance. Although it received the 1994 Aurora Award and the CLA's Young Adult Book Award, *Nobody's Son* does not seem to have received a great deal of popular attention. Juvenile secondary world fantasy in Canada in the nineties was very much an oddity. However, by the turn of the millennium the number of such fantasies began to rise.

The King's Daggers Trilogy (J/YA)

The King's Daggers books by Dave Duncan, *Sir Stalwart* (1999), *The Crooked House* (2000) and *Silvercloak* (2001) are published in the United States. For this reason, Duncan's books are not usually regarded as "Canadian" when schools and libraries are endeavouring to find Canadian content for their shelves. Unlike some other Canadian fantasy and science fiction writers

---

[2] And my *Torrie and the Dragon* (1997); though it was many years of "children don't read fantasy" before the series continued with *Torrie and the Pirate-Queen*, *Torrie and the Firebird*, and *Torrie and the Snake-Prince* (2005-2007).

whose publishers are American, Duncan, who has been publishing adult fantasy novels since the nineteen-eighties and received the 1990 Aurora Award for *West of January* (1989), is not actively promoted within Canada as Canadian.

The world of *The King's Daggers* is that of Duncan's adult *King's Blades* series, a world of late medieval or renaissance society and technology, but without the gunpowder. He offers a carefully-constructed and consistent system of magic, a large geographical and political canvas, and lots of swashbuckling action. Throughout the trilogy, the two main characters, young Sir Stalwart and Sister Emerald of the White Sisters, work undercover for the highest in the land, ensuring the King of Chivial's safety at great risk to themselves. In order for him to ferret out the truth behind a conspiracy to murder the king, Stalwart is expelled from Ironhall, the school that trains the King's Blades, warriors magically bonded to their ward. Emerald is likewise expelled from her order of magic-using women, although unlike Stalwart, she is not a volunteer, but bait for the villains, who want a magic-"sniffing" White Sister free of bonds to the sisterhood. However, after their first adventure, the two become allies, serving the king in full awareness of the risks they run. *The Crooked House* sees them confronting treason, old politics, sorcery, and divided loyalties, while in *Silvercloak* they hunt a mysterious assassin. Emerald shines in this story, disguising herself as a boy to assume an undercover role in the all-male Ironhall as the bullied "Brat" or newest boy. The trilogy ends, satisfyingly, with public royal recognition of their undercover work and heroism.

All the elements of good teen adventure stories are here: action, growing up, politics, intrigue, a hint of romance, and in Emerald and Stalwart, likeable heroes with a great deal of personal integrity. Duncan's world is large and well-developed. The geography, history, the political situation, religious and cosmological background, are all rich, consistent, and convincing in detail.[3] The presence of magic is thoroughly integrated into all aspects of that world; it is not a convenience or an excuse for sudden reversals in

---

[3] Although, like far too many writers, Duncan sticks in baled hay without thinking about it—even a Victorian hay-press seems unlikely for his society's needs, and a mid-twentieth-century baler is technologically out of the question.

the heroes' fortunes, but a consistent factor, without which the stories, and the world in which they take place, could not exist.

A Riddle of Roses (J)

A Riddle of Roses (2000) is a traditional fantasy by Caryl Cude Mullin and her only book to date. It tells the story of a quest set in world created from British folklore, where Arthur, Taliesin, and Avalon are not-too-distant history, the forests hold friendly hermits and ancient magical creatures as well as bandits, and the fairies, although they might have wings, are far from sweet or wish-granting. Meryl, a mabinog or student bard, has been banished for a year from the Hall where such storytellers and singers are trained, as punishment for reading a forbidden book about the adventures of the great bard Taliesin, a book reserved for Masters only. Rather than spend a year doing dull chores, Meryl embarks on a quest for a cauldron said to make whoever drinks from it either mad or a bard. Her journey rapidly becomes entangled with the quests and missions of others, a tree-spirit, a fool, and a practical-joking fairy, the latter inflicted on the party as guide and guard after Meryl makes an enemy of the fairy king and is given a task to perform for him, with the threat of losing her voice if she fails.

The characterization lacks subtlety, relying mainly on caricature of a single trait for its effect. Many of the adventures Meryl has along the way to the end of her quest are, when compared to classic children's secondary world journeys such as those of *The Silver Chair* (1953) or *The Book of Three* (1964), lightweight page-fillers which do not build towards the climax but seem staged merely to break up the journey or illustrate the advent of some new character—though this may be the plot function of such episodes, one should not be consciously aware of it while reading. However, the main thread of the plot holds together throughout the story, carrying in a natural way the book's theme, the need to revitalize art that has lost its creative impulse and become a static tradition. By the end Meryl has learned something of her art and claimed her place as a bard; she has also restored harmony to a disrupted fairy society and reunited one of her companions with a stolen treasure of spiritual significance. The fantasy is the foundation of the story, and though the novel is not one that can be compared in overall literary quality to the works of a writer such as

Alexander, it has charm and internal integrity, and, as a secondary world fantasy from the year 2000, it was venturing where few other Canadian-published novels for younger readers had dared.

Whisperings of Magic (J/YA)

Karleen Bradford is primarily a writer of well-crafted children's historical fiction, with settings both Canadian and, unusual for the Canadian market, medieval European. In *Dragonfire* (1997) and *Whisperings of Magic* (2001) she turned to secondary world fantasy. In these, Bradford concentrates on the coming-of-age of her two main characters, Dahl and Catryn, who must both overcome serious personal weaknesses to achieve their goals. *Dragonfire* is among the few secondary world fantasies for children published in Canada in the nineteen-nineties, and even in it, the hero is pulled from one world to another, where he turns out to be the missing heir to the throne. The world Dahl begins in is not the modern primary world, but a generic, stock-parts medieval one; the place he ends up is very similar, but with the addition of magic. While the first book is Dahl's and follows his self-confrontation and claiming of his kingdom, the second belongs to his friend Catryn. In *Whisperings of Magic*, Dahl is the ruler of the land of Taun and Catryn has become a powerful user of magic, able to take animal form. Her pride and overconfidence put a mission to defeat a new threat to the kingdom at risk. The very fallible characters, who must continually fight to maintain ascendancy over the worst in their natures as they battle dark magic, treason, and dragons, make these stories interesting, but the narrative is humourless and dry in many passages. Though the magic experienced by the characters is carefully constructed and consistently portrayed, the world of Dahl's kingdom of Taun has scant living detail to bring it to life. Standard elements are outlined; at the end, one retains little impression of the world or the life and society of its people, and while reading, one is often left watching from outside as the remote characters walk across a stage, with the result that the story does not succeed in convincing of its reality as one reads.

The Dollmage (YA)

The Dollmage (2001) is a standalone secondary world fantasy by Martine Leavitt, who, as Martine Bates wrote an earlier secondary world fantasy trilogy beginning with *The Dragon's Tapestry* (1992); this was among the earliest Canadian examples of straight secondary world fantasy for young adults. *The Dollmage* is set in a pre-industrial world of isolated, apparently self-governing villages. The narrator is a bitter, angry old woman, the Dollmage of the village of Seekvalley. She is telling the story to the angry villagers at the moment of the story's crisis, as they prepare to stone the young woman Annakey; her aim is to explain to them how they reached this point. The Dollmage's role is to make dolls that have the power to shape people and events. Two girls are born in the village apparently predestined to be the Dollmage's successor; she chooses Renoa because she dislikes Annakey's mother. The Dollmage makes orphaned Annakey's hard life harder, but spoils Renoa, who grows up utterly selfish and arrogant.

The story is a tragedy, redeemed only at the very end. Renoa destroys Annakey's model of the village, which causes a wildfire that destroys the real village and kills Renoa. The villagers have followed the Dollmage's lead in despising and rejecting Annakey, though, and try to stone her, even after they have heard the story the Dollmage tells, although by then the Dollmage has realized that Annakey is destined to lead them and found a new village. The stoning is only averted because the narrator stays behind, offering her own death to atone for Annakey's failure to keep a promise, extracted by force, to marry the man who raped her; the broken promise condemns the girl to death by the village's laws. Despite all the Dollmage's expounding and reinterpreting of the signs around Annakey's birth, which she admits she misinterpreted wilfully, turning the villagers against the girl, the Dollmage never seems to feel she has sins of her own to atone for, and remains a well-rendered self-righteous and repellent character to the end.

The fantasy aspect is handled convincingly and consistently, conveying the claustrophobic, isolated village, the absolute theocratic power the Dollmage wields unchallenged, speaking for God, and the power of the figures the Dollmages shape throughout the story. Characters are shallower than the well-developed magic of the Dollmages, which is gradually revealed through event and detail. No-one, in the narrator's presentation, has any internal life;

they are all observed from outside, a drawback inherent in a first-person narrative with a narrator who holds herself so remote from all other characters. One watches Annakey's sufferings, pitying her but never sharing her life or getting to know her in any intimate way.

The narrator's self-presentation does not take readers into even her own deeper thoughts or emotions; the story is strictly limited to what she might plausibly reveal to the blood-thirsty village mob at the moment of Annakey's intended execution, as she strives once more to manipulate them to her current point of view. However, the narrative's matter of fact portrayal of a relatively simple and limited world allows that to be accepted by the reader as the totality of the narrator's knowledge; one does not, while reading, fall out of the story to wonder about the larger world, about the movements of peoples, the greater cosmology, or who, beyond the village level, decides what God does and does not allow, as one would be likely to do when reading a story with such a setting and a more conventional narrative. In the latter case, the world would seem assembled from a few stock parts, two-dimensional movie sets—the primitive agrarian village, the barbarian horde, a patch of wilderness. As it is, the bitter first-person narrative and the claustrophobic setting work together to create the repressive atmosphere so essential to the story of Annakey's life; the powers of the Dollmage which are shown developing in her and in Renoa are woven firmly into the world, adding, like the narrative style, to the sustaining of literary belief.

On Wings of a Dragon (YA)

Cora Taylor's previous fantasy was typical of Canadian fantasy in the later twentieth century: her *Julie* (see page 14) and *Julie's Secret* featured a contemporary girl with paranormal powers, while *The Doll*, *Ghost Voyages*, and *Ghost Voyages II* (see page 33) were time-travel stories. *On Wings of a Dragon* (2001), in contrast to the weak time-travel story written during the same 2000-2004 period, is a satisfyingly complex secondary world fantasy, following the intersecting lives of two young women. Kour'el awakes imprisoned in a tower with no memory of who she is. She only gradually discovers that she is not human, but a winged girl from a distant land, where some of her people are chosen to work with the Great Ones, immortal dragons. She and her dragon partner, Api'Naga, were ambushed while on a mission; Api'Naga was killed and Kour'el's wings cut off. However, dragons can only be truly killed if their bodies are eaten, so Queen Mariah, the tyrant who rules the land in her ailing husband's name, is feeding Api'Naga's flesh to Kour'el, unaware that this is restoring the girl's wings and helping a tiny resurrected Api'Naga to grow to nearly his original size.

The other main character is Maighdlin, a girl taken as slave labour for the palace. Her grandfather Petaurus and the fiancé of another conscripted girl travel to the capital planning a rescue. Maighdlin's refusal to meekly accept her fate throws her into the midst of critical events, as the queen poisons the king while Kour'el and Api'Naga escape in search of him. A final confrontation of all the main characters reveals that the king was merely a regent, ruling until the rightful heir, Galea, came of age. Galea is Maighdlin, raised by the daughter of Petaurus as her own. In the sequel, *On Wings of Evil* (2005), Queen Mariah returns as a harpy, servant of an evil shape-shifter who is threatening not only Galea's island kingdom, but the land of the dragons and other mainland countries.

The world, with its landscape based on that of Tasmania, is convincing, as are the characters and the well-integrated magic. The interlaced narrative works very well to gradually resolve the various mysteries of identity. Characters are not labelled, but reveal themselves through their actions, as in any good story. The conclusion, with a very uncertain Maighdlin-Galea facing the necessity of restoring a kingdom suffering from years of oppression and misrule, is realistic and in keeping with the world and situation which unfolded through the book. She may be in the position of a lost fairy-tale princess rediscovered, but this is not a fairy-tale world and the duty she assumes is a difficult one, though one which readers will be confident she has the strength, aided by her friends, to cope with. A weak point in the continuing story is the revelation of Maighdlin's identity; nothing is offered in the first two books to explain why she is the rightful heir, or where, in fact, the infant Galea came from, but given the careful and deliberate unveiling of other mysteries so far, this may be revealed in a further book. *On Wings of a Dragon* and its sequel are capable of carrying readers into a richly-imagined and very believable world and story.

The Freyan Trilogy (J/YA)

The third in Linda Smith's *The Freyan Trilogy*, *The Turning Time* (2001) is a sequel to *Wind Shifter* (1995) and *Sea Change* (1999). Aside from fantasy novels for young readers set in this secondary world, Smith has written one real world beginning chapter book and a picture book. *Wind Shifter*, her first novel, was one of very few secondary world fantasies to be published in Canada in the nineties. The trilogy tells the story of a teenage apprentice wizard, Kerstin, whose homeland, Freya, has been threatened with drought by the Uglessians, a race of six-fingers magicians and farmers who live in an impoverished land beyond the mountains. Kerstin is preoccupied with her own resentments and jealousies, particularly of her father's other apprentice. Early in the series this leads her to set off on her own; by *The Turning Time*, she has lived among the Uglessians, matured, and come to understand why they need to alter the wind patterns of the world. It is Kerstin who undertakes the dangerous job, given the prejudice and ignorant hatred directed against the Uglessians, of persuading her own rulers that some degree of the changed weather patterns must be left uncorrected, to prevent widespread drought and famine in Uglessia. Her actions effect great changes in both Uglessian and Freyan society. Those societies are somewhat thinly conceived, without much consideration of how they might actually work—the complexity to be convincing is lacking. The Uglessians are peace-loving, egalitarian, subsistence farmers, the Freyans hierarchical, socially restrictive, and prejudiced against anyone different. There is little depth to the portrayal of either society beyond these traits.

However, other aspects of the world have more life. The past of these two societies causes problems rather than being a simple device of convenience; the plot is fully integrated into the recent political history of the world and the characters' lives are shaped and overturned by both the past and current events. The magic which is so fundamental to the plot and the world from the first book onwards is very well developed from the start, internally consistent and rational throughout, and accordingly, capable of engendering and sustaining literary belief.

Tales of Three Lands trilogy (J/YA)

After her *Freyan Trilogy*, Linda Smith returned to that world to follow the story into a new generation. *The Minstrel's Daughter* (2004) begins the *Tales of Three Lands* trilogy. The young hero, Catrina, leaves her farming village in search of her minstrel father. Times are hard due to drought and in the city of Freyfall she finds herself little better than a beggar. When a spell to find her father, cast by Garth, a magician's apprentice who wants to be a musician, goes wrong, Cat is turned into a real cat. Eventually she and Garth do find her father, only to discover he is working for conspirators who want to stir up enmity between Freyans and Uglessians again, destroying the peace that was reached between the two peoples in the first trilogy. Their attempts to extricate Cat's father from the plot bring them into contact with Talisa, who is the hero of the next book. By the end, Cat has foiled an assassination attempt that was meant to start a war; she has ensured that the peace, for the moment, will remain unbroken. *Talisa's Song* (2005), picks up the story from the point of view of Talisa, a young Uglessian musician who defies her family to follow her calling, becoming involved with a Freyan boy and an emerging class conflict in Freya. It is also an example of a secondary world culture considering primary world issues: the growing of cash crops for the Freyans will make some of the poor but egalitarian Uglessians wealthy while reducing others to a state where they cannot support themselves, destroying the self-sufficiency of the culture—a situation now widespread in the developing world, as people cease farming to feed themselves and their communities and turn to growing cash crops to provide cheap, out-of-season products for Europe and North America.

As with the early trilogy, in *Tales of Three Lands* the magic is consistent and is woven into the recent political history of the world; it causes problems rather than being a simple device of convenience, while the stories are told with humour and suspense. Characters are well-developed; Talisa in particular stands out as a young hero who develops the courage to take a stand for what she believes, though this means opposing and angering members of her own family. While many aspects of the world remain sketchy, it grows in depth and realism as Smith explores it further, fleshing out the somewhat generic landscapes and cultures of the first series into a fuller reality.

Captain Jenny and the Sea of Wonders and *The Star-Glass* (J/YA)

Captain Jenny and the Sea of Wonders (2001) is the second of Duncan Thornton's books set in this secondary world; the trilogy contains his only novels to date. The first story, *Kalifax* (1999), follows the adventures of Tom, a boy who takes part on an expedition of exploration. *Kalifax* is a voyage through the North-West Passage, with the perils of snow-goblins added to the danger of being ice-bound and starving or freezing to death. Although it makes reference to events of the first book, *Captain Jenny* can be read on its own. In it, Tom's friend Jenny, a "proud and wordy" fisher-girl, sets out on a quest to sail the Sea of Wonders Lost and Found in search of the Lost City that sank below the waters an age before.

Jenny and her crew have many adventures in the perilous and magic-ridden Sea of Wonders, recalling but not merely repeating those of Odysseus. When after many trials she reaches the Lost City, Jenny must decide whether or not to wake the sleeping inhabitants by ringing a bell, an episode that recalls Digory and Polly facing a similar choice in the city of Charn in C.S. Lewis' *The Magician's Nephew* (1956). Jenny believes the reviving of the City and the establishment of a new age of wonders to be the object of her quest, but wisely mulling over the words of an oracle and applying logic to the reading of a series of pictures on the temple walls, she realizes she may have interpreted both wrongly. What she has seen of the sleeping inhabitants increases her uncertainty. It suddenly seems possible that the restoration of the City will begin a new age of terror and desolation. It is an extremely well done moment of quiet drama. She chooses not to ring the bell, and a great wave crashes over the city, sinking it again. Jenny and her companion, the mortally-injured Cook, have to swim. The Cook's eventual death is a powerful piece of writing on a subject often handled in children's books only through safe conventions.

Jenny is an endearing and credible young hero: she is an experienced sailor and quick-thinking explorer, but she is also a child unused in leading others. She matures through the book, learning from the crew and her own experience. In addition, like many intelligent and widely-read children, she suffers from an urge to hold forth on anything and everything at the slightest excuse, which provides some of the book's comedy as well as being a practical means of explaining both Jenny's world and new words and concepts. The major child characters are well-developed, while most of the adults who play significant secondary roles are portrayed as figures emerging out of legend, with a stark simplicity that, though not the psychological realism of the modern novel, is not flat either. The various ships' crews largely act as a chorus, a group entity moving in the background with individuals distinguished to the audience by a single trait.

The Star-Glass (2003) continues the adventures of Tom and Jenny the Fisher-Girl. This time they are on an expedition to explore a new land across the sea, in the face of coming darkness, the "Long Night" of war and plague. The Captain sails west in the *Volantrix*, to see if the prohibition on settlers in the Vastlands, a mysterious land with which the people of Tom's home of Landsend have some trade, has been lifted. There are references to Tolkien's mythology, in passing mentions of the Elves having sailed west as well. Tom and Jenny sail as ensigns on the *Volantrix*, and their explorations into the interior of the Vastlands leads to many encounters with great natural and supernatural dangers. In the end, the people of Landsend do cross the ocean, the expedition, through great courage and sacrifice, having found a new home for them in the Homely Country by the Hidden Sea. The book has an elegiac quality found in authors such as Tolkien and Rosemary Sutcliff (author of *The Eagle of the Ninth*, *The Lantern Bearers*, and many other outstanding works of historical fiction for young people), who wrote of the end of one age and the beginning of another, and of the need to preserve what was good of the past: Tom's father makes a library in the new land, to preserve the knowledge of the east. There are also those, like Jenny's ancient godmother, who choose to remain in Landsend, defying the coming darkness to the end. More so than the first two, *The Star-Glass* is by times dark, poetic, moving, mysterious, and awe-evoking. It is not a book that will appeal to everyone, particularly not those for whom reading is a chore or who want a quick, light entertainment, but it is a story that can linger in the imagination and which will repay more than one reading, and that is one of the earmarks of good fantasy.

Thornton's stories are told with convincing and well-researched detail in nautical matters, a wealth of invention, and a delicate balance of humour and seriousness, action, thought, and suspense. Through his obvious pleasure in language, he also reacts against the belief held by some that vocabulary must be "dumbed down" when writing for children. These are not books for the struggling reader or the child put off by the unfamiliar in vocabulary and narrative approach; they are books to challenge and expand the imaginative horizons. Throughout, Thornton deftly weaves together magic and practicalities to create a very real and dangerous secondary world that is full of wonder and mythic potential. His world also echoes our own quite closely, capturing the romance, heroism, and tragedy of the days of early exploration and, in the third volume, issues of colonization as well. All of this may stimulate curiosity and further reading of the sorts of nonfiction—history, explorers' accounts, travellers' tales—which underlie the creation of Thornton's world. The trilogy is outstanding and original fantasy, which deserves to become a Canadian classic. Few writers have even attempted to mythologize and create a living romance of the Canadian landscape as so many British writers have done for their land; Thornton, in reflecting in his secondary world aspects of our land, not so much in a clear mirror as in a shifting and transforming forest pool, succeeds.

The Phantom Queen (YA)

Although Ven Begamudré has written several collections of poetry and short stories for adults, *The Phantom Queen* is his only work for children and his only fantasy. The plot of *The Phantom Queen* (2002) has the feel of legend to it. It is the story of Nevsky, a young prophet, wise man, and magic-worker, whose knowledge is gained by passing through a cave into another world to confront trials which are never described in any detail, but from which he always returns wiser, though often older in spirit and physically battered. Nevsky's companion, at once an independent creature and the wise man's own spirit, is the shapeshifting Sovah, who is most often seen as an owl. The setting is the little kingdom of Mir, a society based largely on that of early medieval or Kievan Russia. Nevsky adopts Ekho, a baby girl rejected by the villagers after he saved her soul from Dhiavol, the devil. Satan is very much present and active in Mir, as he is in many fairy-tales. When Dhiavol nearly destroys Mir through civil war between the twin princes, only Ekho, now a young woman betrothed to Nevsky, can bring peace through her singing. First she must journey through the cave herself to acquire Nevsky's wisdom.

Ekho's otherworldly journey is where the story falters and fails to convince. Her encounter in a world of reversed colours with a painter about to be executed, who is both Nevsky and his familiar Sovah, is trivial as a spirit-quest in search of wisdom, too shallow to explain her or Nevsky's enlightenment and transformation; little is shown to have changed in Ekho or in her perception of the world, though we are assured she has changed, gaining Nevsky's power and the ability to bring peace to the land.

After her return from this spirit-journey the lovers part, to meet again only in the framing narrative, where it is revealed that the old minstrel telling the story of Nevsky and Ekho to a royal audience in a distant southern land is Nevsky, and the elderly peace-bringing queen is Ekho. This two-layered framing story, with its reflections on impatient and over-knowing youth from the perspective of mellower age, sometimes adds to the story and sometimes seems an unnecessarily rambling digression.

However, Begamudré succeeds in creating the feeling of another time and place, another culture, providing rich detail that is never overdone. In Nevsky, he presents a character who remains very human while retaining an air of mystery and of legendary greatness. He offers a convincingly medieval blend of elements of Orthodox Christianity and folk-magic that on the whole succeeds. The story's weakness lies not in its fantasy, but in the bones of its plot, wherein the central and transforming crisis in the life of the hero Ekho is an anticlimax.

The Blue Roan Child (J/YA)

Jamieson Findlay's only book to date is *The Blue Roan Child* (2002). It tells the story of the orphaned stable-girl Syeira, who frees a captive mare of the ancient, intelligent Arva breed to find her twin colts, which have been sold to a neighbouring tyrant, Ran of Stormsythe. The mare, Arwin, communicates emotion and images through breathing scent pictures into Syeira's mind, an original premise which Findlay renders very convincingly. As they travel, the girl becomes concerned with her own identity, her future and past, for a time succumbing to, but overcoming, the temptation of a drug which lets her exist almost entirely in memories of past happiness. Ran's country is torn by civil war, and the various adult allies and enemies Syeira encounters on her journey there are all, one way or another, scarred by this. Some have become stronger, finding new depths of personal integrity and new strength; others are taking the easy road of capitulation to tyranny. For all of them, involvement with Syeira and Arwin becomes as transforming as it is for the girl and horse. Syeira's passage through Stormsythe coincides with and adds to the transformation of that society by revolution; Syeira, who has discovered her father and been the cause of both his redemption and heroic death, continues her journey, now one towards adulthood as an itinerant master-horsewoman, with the Arva horses. The tyrant Ran is the only poorly developed character; the weak allegory he tells about himself being stripped of his childhood on the island of nightmares seems, when compared to the less central but more naturally developed characters, a not very effective attempt to give his character depth and to account for his cruelty and love of things mechanical.

The Blue Roan Child features an unconventional relationship between the characters of girl and horse; it is Arwin, the mare, who is the driving will on the quest, while Syeira is merely a companion, tolerated because she is useful, though she remains the one who must make decisions and come up with plans. As horse and human come to depend on one another more, greater trust and friendship grow between them. The development of Syeira's character is convincing and realistic: her initial decision to free the mare is impulsive and unconsidered, while her true moral struggle and growth come over the course of the journey. Although some elements of the book, in particular Ran's island of nightmares and the flying horses (which show up rather suddenly in order to aid the rebels), seem poorly-integrated into the whole and have the jarring tang of mere convenience, the prose is excellent, the plot has plenty of action and suspense, and the world through which Syeira and Arwin travel is portrayed in depth and is always convincingly real. *The Blue Roan Child* is a strong secondary world fantasy.

The Estorian Chronicles (J)

Nikki Tate is the author of a number of children's books about contemporary girls, mostly horse-stories, as well as two good historical fiction beginning chapter books, *Jo's Triumph* (2002) and *Jo's Journey* (2006). She ventured into fantasy with *The Cave of Departure* (2002) and *The Battle for Carnillo* (2003). The hero, Dominique, is exiled from his people for failing to tell a story at his coming-of-age rite. He leaves his stagnant, restrictive society for a larger world, encounters many dangers, a few friends and allies, and finds himself in the midst of a rebellion against the tyrant of Carnillo. Stories, prophecies, and the beliefs of the rebels all point to Dominique as a destined hero, but the story itself fails to show him either growing into or fulfilling this role. Dominique demonstrates no sign of any ability to lead, plan, or inspire. Even by the end of the second book he has revealed little evidence of being able to act decisively and independently, or to think and plan ahead. He remains throughout a passive character who reacts to events but displays little initiative or even will of own. The supporting cast seems just that, flat characters invented to fill necessary roles surrounding Dominique, to cause him problems or push him along through the plot.

Unlike Tate's well-written *Jo* books, with their nicely-balanced character development, action, and researched background, *The Estorian Chronicles* seem laboured, the world unconvincing. Rather than bringing the invented cultures, landscapes, and creatures to life, the cataloguing of every minor detail and the over-description of the simplest of actions dulls any illusion of reality such description is intended to create, blanketing everything in a fog of words. The continual references to the storytelling lore of Dominique's Estorian people fail to complement, accentuate, or foreshadow anything in the plot, and thus become only further clutter. The characters never develop beyond genre stereotypes— the näive boy thrust out into the world on his own, the feisty female sidekick who takes him under her wing, the wise elder who provides guidance and dies—but the characters have nothing more to them than these roles. As with the plot and the elements of the world, one never loses the feeling that the *function* of the characters came first. This is not so much window-dressing to decorate an instructional story, as a novel mechanically following some preconceived formula of what a secondary world fantasy novel is supposed to have in it.

Airborn (J/YA)

Following his animal fantasy series about bats (see page 85), Kenneth Oppel turned to alternate world fantasy with *Airborn* (2004). The setting is a variant of our own world, one in which most intercontinental shipping is carried by airships using the fictitious gas hydrium. Matt Cruse is a cabin boy on the luxury airship *Aurora*. Matt and a wealthy passenger, Kate de Vries, become allies in proving her explorer grandfather's observations of batlike, flying panthers (cloud cats) were not the product of madness. When the *Aurora* is damaged in an attack by the pirate Szpirglas, it sets down for repairs on an uncharted island. While the crew makes repairs, Kate and Matt find a cloud cat skeleton, and then a cat with a damaged wing. They also discover, too late to avoid capture, that the island is Szpirglas's base. Kate and Matt escape; their fight to overcome the pirates and free the crew and passengers is one of outstanding high drama and tragedy.

Airborn works on many levels. It is not just a tale of adventure and fantastic discovery, but a story of two young people hampered in their ambitions by the restrictions of society. The world has changed since the early days of airships and it is no longer easy to work one's way through the ranks as Matt aspires to do; although women can attend university, it is not considered the proper pursuit for a well-born young lady, and Kate's parents have no sympathy for her ambitions. Both Matt and Kate must go to great lengths to pursue their goals. Kate achieves success in her mission to prove the cloud cats real and wins her parents' permission to attend university, but recognizes that by much of the scientific community she is not taken seriously, her cloud cat skeleton and slides suspected of being faked. She still has much to prove, to win the respect of the field she has chosen to enter. Matt, on the other hand, is able to attend the academy, thanks to reward money offered for the pirates, and finds his dreams of becoming an officer at last within his reach. The delicate beginning of romance between Kate and Matt is handled with great naturalness and humour, a fact of their friendship and a part of its tensions. Matt's final acceptance of the reality of his father's death enables him to overcome his almost phobic reaction to being on solid ground.

The main check to literary belief (other than the addition to the periodic table of an element lighter than hydrogen yet complex enough to have an organic smell) is the impossibility of a mammal surviving alone from the moment of birth. This is what the crippled cloud cat discovered by Matt and Kate, whose birth, fall, and abandonment by its mother were witnessed by Kate's grandfather and recorded in his diary, seems to have done.

The sequel, *Skybreaker* (2005), continues to develop both the history of this world and the biology of the mysterious higher reaches of the atmosphere, capturing the excitement of the era of great explorations along with the "boy's adventure" stories of the early twentieth century, full of daring escapes, exotic settings, and villainous criminals foiled by youthful heroes.

Airborn and *Skybreaker* offer a convincing literary reality, in which young protagonists confront and overcome great challenges and dangers, while moving into maturity. The fully-realized world is vaster than the scope of the story, in which much more remains to be explored. *Airborn* received the 2004 Governor-General's Award for children's literature; does the fact that a few years after Slade's *Dust* won the 2001 award (see page 62), a thoroughly-integrated fantasy (which could not possibly be mistaken for the more "respectable" genre of Canlit) received this prestigious award suggest an increasing respect for fantasy literature in Canada?

Summoned to Destiny
(Realms of Wonder series) (YA)

The first in a series of anthologies called *Realms of Wonder*, *Summoned to Destiny* (2004) is edited by Canadian science fiction author Julie E. Czerneda, whose numerous adult novels, published in the United States, are very highly regarded. This Canadian-published collection for teens contains eight short stories, six of them by Canadians. The stories appeal to a variety of tastes, but all are secondary world fantasy, all are uniformly well written, their worlds well created and thoroughly realized. Jane Paniccia's story of Shen, "Offering of Trust", who in the aftermath of a war between humans and red dragons, accepts the burden of becoming a Protector and takes on part of the soul of a benevolent golden dragon, is a good representative of the type of story to be found here. Another is Karina Sumner-Smith's "A Prayer of Salt and Sand". In this, the hero Asha has five times performed unsuccessfully the ritual vigil and prayers that should connect her with the goddess Narelle, who sacrificed her life to save her people from a rising sea. Despite this failure, Asha has always been convinced that she, sole survivor of a village destroyed by storm-surge, should be special. Deciding on her own that she has no right to remain among the priestesses of the religious community in which she was raised, Asha leaves in a small boat, sailing aimlessly while trying to think what to do with her life. However, in trying to save a girl from murder, she is finally able to open herself to her goddess; Asha's willingness to sacrifice herself both makes her worthy and connects her with the goddess who was once a human girl. Though the theme is simple, it is an enduring one, and through the character of Asha it is explored in a way that gives it renewed impact.

In this collection there is neither window-dressing nor genre cliché. The stories will meet the demands of serious adult fantasy readers as well as the teens for whom they are written. All the stories in the collection are of young people expanding into maturity. The heroes, male and female, realize and create their destinies, or take the first conscious steps towards fulfilling their fates. Some are stories by established names in the field, such as Ed Greenwood and Michelle West, while others are by newcomers. Many of the stories, although arriving at a satisfying conclusion, could stand as the first episode in a novel; the characters and the worlds all have the structure to bear a larger story, and many of them leave the reader wanting to know what happens to the hero next. The second *Realms of Wonder* anthology, *Fantastic Companions* (2005) is also edited by Czerneda, and again contains a selection of excellent fantasy short stories, a number of them by Canadians. As the title suggests, the stories in the second collection share the theme of animal or mythical-creature companions; most are secondary world fantasy and most are tantalizingly suggestive of a larger story about to happen. All the stories in these two collections edited by Czerneda are outstanding examples of what secondary world fantasy can and should be.[4]

SECONDARY WORLD FANTASY creates another world. It may be quite similar to our own or differ wildly. It offers unlimited scope for exploration; imagination can be given free rein. *But*, it must abide by its own rules. The world must be internally consistent, to be believable. Secondary world fantasy (along with the secondary worlds of dual-world fantasy), is in some ways the most challenging to do well and the easiest to do badly. Some secondary world fantasy aimed at young readers simply plunders adult fantasy for a glittery window-dressing, the way the equivalent in science fiction for children pulls its genre-veneer from television, to create something that is both bad science fiction or fantasy and bad children's literature, with stock characters, plots, and props. Such superficial works entice by their novelty those who have not read much good speculative fiction for children or adults, but rarely stand up to rereading. In fact, the weak and shallow often seem to be more favourably regarded by non-fantasy readers, because they are easier to grasp—everything is familiar, requiring no effort, consisting as it does of cardboard cut-outs and clichés familiar from popular culture. Although examples of the latter approach to secondary world fantasy will probably continue to be found in Canadian (and international) publishing so long as some believe fantasy need only be formulaic to sell, the majority of Canadian secondary world fantasies of the 2000-2004 period were being taken seriously by their creators. Particularly outstanding are the works of Findlay, Thornton, Duncan, Taylor, and Oppel, who have all created very rich, distinctive, and fully-realized

---

[4] The third *Realms of Wonder* collection is of equal quality, although it does not belong in a discussion of secondary world fantasy. *Mythspring: From the Lyrics and Legends of Canada* (2006), is edited by Czerneda and Genevieve Kierans; the stories included, by authors such as Charles de Lint and Alison Baird, take Canadian songs and tales as their inspiration; most are fantasy, with one or two science fiction stories as well, and have some form of Canadian setting.

worlds, through which to tell well-crafted stories. In most of these, believable heroes do act to change not only themselves, but the lives of those around them. Findlay, and the new writers found in the collections edited by Czerneda, suggest that there is much more good secondary and alternate world fantasy to come; a new generation of authors is just beginning to find its feet. Even though Canadian publishers have only recently begun to appreciate stories set in secondary and alternate worlds, this subset of fantasy literature seems now to be making a promising, if late, start.

X
BEYOND WINDOW-DRESSING

CERTAIN TRENDS IN CANADIAN children's fantasy emerge in such a study as this, which are worthy of further consideration. Why, for instance, in these stories published between 2000 and 2004, are there only about half as many male heroes as female ones? Is it attributable to the fact that there are almost twice as many female authors as male? (And why is that? Are women more likely to write for children? Are they, given the difficulties of earning a living as a Canadian writer, more likely to be able combine writing with part-time work, or with a higher-paid spouse's security of pension and medical insurance than men are?) One surely cannot say that women more properly and naturally write about female characters and men about male; although Carol Shields was once praised on the CBC's "Morningside" for daringly using a male protagonist in her novel *Larry's Party* (1997), any examination of speculative fiction, not to mention fiction in general, reveals rather a large number of men writing female heroes and women writing males. The reaction of that interviewer to a narrative choice that was hardly an innovation is typical of the perception in the current "lit crit" atmosphere that male and female are separated by a wide gulf, and that only the exceptional imagination is permitted to bridge it.

A more likely cause for the fact that only just over a third of children's fantasy heroes are male may be that many publishers, particularly in Canada, are keen to have female heroes, perhaps in an effort to "correct" the perceived imbalances of twentieth-century children's literature, but this does gender equality no service. At a time when there are so many complaints about boys not reading, and when every year the crop of books promoted as appealing to boys consists primarily of sports and school stories, it is obvious that more imaginative stories with heroic male leads are needed. Boys read stories with female heroes; girls read ones with male. Everybody, however, does at times want to imagine a heroic role for someone very like him- or herself, and gender is the primary identity in our society, the first group identity (other than that of family) we are taught we belong to. Everyone needs to be able to imaginatively experience being someone else, but sometimes it is good to recognize a crucial element of yourself in a character, too. Girls did hunger for more of Eowyn's brief period on centre stage as a warrior in *The Lord of the Rings*; C.J. Cherryh's Morgaine (*Gate of Ivrel*, 1976), was a revelation and a relief to female science fiction and fantasy readers of the seventies (despite the cover), and Robin McKinley's Harry and Aerin (*The Blue Sword*, 1982; *The Hero and the Crown*, 1985) and Tamora Pierce's Alanna (*Alanna: The First Adventure*, 1983) were first read with a feeling of "Yessss, at last!" by girls of the eighties. But that is no reason that in the twenty-first century, strong male protagonists should be in such short supply in Canadian children's fantasy, particularly in good secondary and dual-world fantasy, which offer the most striking alternative to real-world stories for those who want something to carry them away. Children's literature in the twenty-first century should have matured sufficiently to offer a balanced range of heroes, instead of replacing one inequality with another.

The passivity of the protagonists in some fantasies is also an obvious, and worrying, tendency. The main characters in a number of the stories examined here do not dominate the action; they merely enter a story and tag along, witnessing events and reacting to them, but not precipitating them or attempting to change their course. They take no responsibility upon themselves. In the worst cases, the hero seems merely an observer, a stand-in for the reader, as though the story's creator was excited by the idea of fantasy but could not imagine truly living it, only observing, as if watching a movie. Are the imaginations of the rising generation so stunted by passive entertainments that readers (and even authors) are losing the ability to imagine themselves into the active roles of a story?

Similar to passive heroes are passive plots, in which events conspire to spare the heroes their most compelling role: that of people forced to make painful, life-altering choices, of having to act at some cost to themselves to change the world. These heroes who avoid sacrifice and violent conflict are not generally shown to be individuals who have consciously adopted non-violence as a philosophy, who are willing to suffer and die in their determination to eschew violence. They are merely characters whose stories unfold without encountering situations in which defending or advancing their cause demands more than moderate hardship. The crucible is never hot enough to reveal their mettle. The heroes of passive plots may be the victims of supernatural evil, or of human oppression, and they may take a stand for or against something, but circumstances always permit them to avoid conflicts that would challenge the heroes or their beliefs. They are never pushed to their limits. Crises in such stories are often resolved without conflict or true risk; an emotional plea is enough to persuade those in power to reconsider. Wishes for a better world, perhaps, but if the heroes never have to risk anything that matters, if they never have to make critical decisions with the possibility of failure or suffering or even death for themselves and others as a consequence, but are conveniently allowed to avoid any extremity of conflict, the story not only lacks dramatic impact, it is reduced to a safe game, playtime rather than reality. Victory, over enemies, over evil, or over oneself, is trivialized. Such a story will not lead readers to consider very deeply the choices the heroes have faced, nor will vicarious participation in such stories provide any guidance for their own moral trials.

Canadian-published fantasy, compared with the best of contemporary fantasy published for both children and teens in Britain and the United States in the late twentieth and early twenty-first centuries (Pratchett, Jones, Alexander, Nix, Jacques, Gaiman...), often seems simple. Worlds tend to be thinner. Plots follow one storyline, not several. Longer storylines do not arch over and weave through the single-volume plots of multi-volume series. Both language and ideas are less complex. In particular, books for children (as opposed to teens) can feel reined in, hobbled, and the result is that they seem thin. Fantasy for teens shows greater improvement in quality than fantasy for children; this is at least partly due to the fact that books for younger readers, more constrained in length and often in vocabulary, are a more difficult medium in which to produce good fantasy, which requires the development of the unfamiliar and complex. Thus, perhaps, the reliance upon stock plots and worlds. However, it is perfectly

BEYOND WINDOW-DRESSING?

possible to write rich fantasy for children. *The Princess and the Goblin* (1872) and *Five Children and It* (1902) to *The Midnight Folk* (1927), *The Hobbit* (1937), *The Chronicles of Narnia* (1950-1956), *The Weirdstone of Brisingamen* (1960), *The Chronicles of Prydain* (1964-1968), *The Dark is Rising* (1965-1977), *The Lives of Christopher Chant* (1988), *The Ragwitch* (1990), *Only You Can Save Mankind* (1992), *Island of the Aunts* (1999), *The Seventh Tower* (2000-2001), *Coraline* (2002), *The Pinhoe Egg* (2006), and *The Keys to the Kingdom* (2003-) all demonstrate this. Although there is a need for books suitable for children with difficulties in reading, the whole canon need not be geared down to that level—must not be, if it is to be an enduring literature rather than a mere reader, as thin and usefully plodding as *Mr. Whiskers* or *Magic and Make Believe*, two of the regrettably now-discarded readers of the seventies. In Canada, schools play a role in this weakening of children's literature by their rejection of readers—texts specifically designed for reading instruction—which built up vocabulary and patterns of language in carefully advancing steps. Instead of providing stories and information which children are free to read as they choose—exploring at their own pace, stretching their imaginations, their vocabularies, their minds and their horizons—it is now expected that juvenile fiction and non-fiction should take up the burden of being a remedy for failed literacy teaching policies. This is not the job of a novel. (Which is not to say, as has been pointed out repeatedly, that a fantasy, or any novel, cannot teach; there are few good books which one can read without learning something, if only about oneself.)

By the emphasis on purchasing only "useful" books, that is, ones that will not be "too difficult" for the ever-decreasing literacy of the "average reader" and which will preferably be suitable for the "emergent" or the struggling reader to whom books are heavy labour rather than pleasure and excitement, and on purchasing books which have an obvious purpose and curricular application, the educational system contributes significantly to the tendency of many publishers to seek children's books that are primarily utilitarian and "average" in all senses. Fiction for the school library is still, by and large, judged not by its literary merits, its value as story and good prose, but by its Canadian-ness and its didactic value. Great writers of even the relatively recent past, such as

Lloyd Alexander, Rosemary Sutcliff, Arthur Ransome, and Susan Cooper, are weeded and discarded, because they do not meet these qualifications and because there is a perception that children will not read "old" books, by which some in the educational system mean anything written before 2000.

These are points which any further study of the state of Canadian children's fantasy literature needs to take into consideration. However, to return to the original question posed here, has Canadian children's literature, at the opening of the new millennium, moved beyond treating fantasy as mere window-dressing?

That seems to depend on the type of fantasy. Time-travel was one of the most common fantasy types in twentieth century Canadian children's literature, but the time-travel was always a device to deliver a history lesson or show a character becoming reconciled to some situation in the present through learning family history. In the period from 2000 to 2004, that approach remains unchanged. Time-travel in Canadian literature is still window-dressing tacked on, sugar for the medicine, to make historical fiction "easy" and "accessible" to the modern child, assumed to be unable to make an imaginative leap into the past without a contemporary guide, or else it is a means for a protagonist, usually an unhappy one, to come to appreciate family history and reconcile him- or herself with the problems of everyday life.

In contrast, fantasy set in the primary world has grown strong, with a number of Canadian authors writing first-rate books in which the fantastic is fully integrated into the primary world. "Speculative fantasy", mixing elements of fantasy and science fiction, is a new field of Canadian fantasy, and although, like primary world fantasy, it can lend itself to being used in a slapdash fashion or can obscure bad writing under a window-dressing of fantasy because of the "fantasy doesn't have to make sense" attitude, it is by and large another very strong area of Canadian juvenile fantasy writing.

Historical fantasy and the re-imagining of traditional or long-familiar tales as novels are likewise aspects of fantasy not found in Canada until the nineties, but in the new century they are becoming more common, and are generally well-done, with the fantasy fully-integrated into a well-written story. Animal fantasy has improved immensely, with at least one Canadian author leaving a lasting imprint on the genre.

In dual-world fantasy, some Canadian authors have written good novels with fully-realized secondary worlds, but others are still using the device of a primary world protagonist discovering a Destiny in a highly derivative or assembled-from-stock-parts secondary world to give an appearance of novelty to a poorly-plotted and only superficially imaginative story, and that veneer of fantasy seems still to be rendering ill-crafted literature acceptable by offering an excuse for its poor quality: "It's only fantasy." Secondary and alternate world fantasy can and does suffer the same treatment at the hands of poor fantasists as dual-world stories, but a strong body of good, fully-realized secondary world novels exists at the start of the twenty-first century, while in the twentieth there were, until the nineties, next to none. The promise shown by young writers in the *Realms of Wonder* anthologies is evidence that in secondary world fantasy, the heartland of the modern fantasy genre, Canadian juvenile literature has moved beyond window-dressing.

Canada still has a long way to go to be regarded internationally as possessed of a national literature producing excellent children's fantasy, but the potential now exists for an author capable of having the impact on the genre of a Diana Wynne Jones, a Susan Cooper or a Lloyd Alexander, a Terry Pratchett or a Garth Nix, to be published in Canada. Much new Canadian children's fantasy has been published since 2004, some of it by new writers who were still unpublished during the time-period examined in this study. It is probably fair to say that since 2004, the amount of children's fantasy published in Canada has continued to increase, and the literary quality, if the trends observed here are anything to go by, on the whole to improve. However, Canada is a small market and even though Canadian publishers do distribute in the United States, such sales are a tiny drop in the sea of American books. Given the unlikelihood of a Canadian-published children's fantasy, whatever its quality, ever attracting enough attention to guarantee widespread international distribution, it seems likely that any Canadian author with the potential to be counted among the greats of the genre will, like Australian Nix, have to be picked up by an American or British publisher to achieve that recognition.

BIBLIOGRAPHY

i. Canadian Fiction

Baird, Alison. *The Dragon's Egg*. Richmond Hill: Scholastic Canada, 1994.
—. *The Hidden World*. Toronto: Viking, 1999.
—. *The Wolves of Woden*. Toronto: Penguin, 2001.
—. *The Witches of Willowmere*. Toronto: Penguin Canada, 2002.
—. *The Warding of Willowmere*. Toronto: Penguin Canada, 2004.
—. *The Stone of the Stars*. New York : Warner Aspect, 2004.
—. *Wyrd of Willowmere*. Toronto: Penguin Canada, 2005.
Bates, Martine. (Martine Leavitt). *The Dragon's Tapestry*. Red Deer: Red Deer College Press, 1992.
—. *The Prism Moon*. Red Deer: Red Deer Press, 1993.
—. *The Taker's Key*. Red Deer: Red Deer Press, 1998.
Bedard, Michael. *Redwork*. Toronto: Lester and Orpen Dennys, 1990.
Begamudré, Ven. *The Phantom Queen*. Regina: Coteau, 2002. Berton, Pierre. *The Secret World of Og*. Toronto: McClelland and Stewart, 1961.
Bishop, Mary Harelkin. *Tunnels of Time*. Regina: Coteau Books, 2000.
—. *Tunnels of Terror*. Regina: Coteau Books, 2001.
—. *Tunnels of Treachery*. Regina: Coteau Books, 2003.
—. *Tunnels of Tyranny*. Regina: Coteau Books, 2005.
Blum, Vicki. *Wish Upon a Unicorn*. Markham: Scholastic Canada, 1999.
—. *The Shadow Unicorn*. Markham: Scholastic Canada, 2000.
—. *The Land Without Unicorns*. Markham: Scholastic Canada, 2001.
—. *A Gathering of Unicorns*. Markham: Scholastic Canada, 2003.
—. *The Mermaid Secret*. Markham: Scholastic Canada, 2004.
Bow, Patricia. *The Bone Flute*. Victoria: Orca Book Publishers, 2004.
Bradford, Karleen. *Dragonfire*. Toronto: HarperCollins Canada, 1997.
—. *Whisperings of Magic*. Toronto: HarperCollins Canada, 2001.
Buchan, John. *Lake of Gold*. Toronto: Musson Book Company, 1941. (UK: *The Long Traverse*. London: Hodder and Stoughton, 1941.)
Buffie, Margaret. *The Watcher*. Toronto: Kids Can, 2000.
—. *The Seeker*. Toronto: Kids Can, 2002.
—. *The Finder*. Toronto: Kids Can, 2004.
Ciddor, Anna. *Runestone*. Georgetown Publishers, 2004.
—. *Wolfspell*. Georgetown Publishers, 2004.
Clark, Catherine Anthony. *The Golden Pine Cone*. Toronto: Macmillan, 1950.
—. *The Sun Horse*. Toronto: Macmillan, 1951.
—. *The One-Winged Dragon*. Toronto: Macmillan, 1955.
—. *The Silver Man*. Toronto: Macmillan, 1958.
—. *The Diamond Feather*. Toronto: Macmillan, 1962.
—. *The Hunter and the Medicine Man*. Toronto: Macmillan, 1966.
Cox, Palmer. *The Brownies: Their Book*. New York: The Century Co., 1887.

(London: T. Fisher Unwin, 1887.)
—. *Another Brownie Book.* New York: Century Co., 1890. London: Unwin, 1890.
—. *The Brownies At Home.* New York: Century Co., 1893. London: Unwin, 1893.
—. *The Brownies Around the World.* New York: Century, 1894. London: Unwin, 1894.
—. *The Brownies Through the Union.* New York: Century, 1895. London: Unwin, 1895.
—. *Brownie Year Book.* New York: McLoughlin Bros., 1895.
—. *The Brownies Abroad.* New York: Century, 1899. London: Unwin, 1899.
—. *The Brownies in the Philippines.* New York: Century, 1904. London: Unwin, 1904.
—. *Brownie Clown of Brownie Town.* New York: Century, 1908.
—. *The Brownies' Latest Adventures.* New York: Century, 1910. London: Unwin, 1910.
—. *The Brownies Many More Nights.* New York: Century, 1913.
—. *The Brownies and Prince Florimel.* New York: Century, 1918.
Czerneda, Julie E. Ed. *Summoned to Destiny.* Markham: Fitzhenry & Whiteside, 2004
—. Ed. *Fantastic Companions.* Markham: Fitzhenry & Whiteside, 2005.
Czerneda, Julie E. & Genevieve Kierans. Eds. *Mythspring: From the Lyrics and Legends of Canada.* Red Deer: Red Deer Press, 2006.
de Lint, Charles. *The Riddle of the Wren.* New York: Ace, 1984.
—. *The Harp of the Grey Rose.* New York: Avon, 1985.
—. *Jack the Giant-Killer.* New York: Ace, 1987.
—. *Wolf Moon.* New York: New American Library, 1988.
—. *The Dreaming Place.* New York: Atheneum, 1990.
—. *Waifs and Strays.* New York: Viking, 2002.
—. *The Riddle of the Wren.* New York: Firebird, 2002.
—. *The Harp of the Grey Rose.* New York: Firebird, 2004.
—. *Wolf Moon.* New York: Firebird, 2004.
—. *The Blue Girl.* New York: Viking, 2004.
Duncan, Dave. *West of January.* New York: Del Rey, 1989.
—. *Sir Stalwart.* New York: Avon, 1999.
—. *The Crooked House.* New York: Avon, 2000.
—. *Silvercloak.* New York: Avon, 2001.
Fast, A.D. *The Mystery of the Medieval Coin.* St. Catharine's: Vanwell, 2004.
Findlay, Jamieson. *The Blue Roan Child.* Toronto: Doubleday Canada, 2002.
Foon, Dennis. *The Dirt Eaters.* Toronto : Annick Press, 2003.
—. *Freewalker.* Toronto: Annick Press, 2004.
—. *The Keeper's Shadow.* Toronto: Annick Press, 2006.
Goobie, Beth. *Flux.* Victoria: Orca Book Publishers, 2004.
—. *Fixed.* Victoria: Orca Book Publishers, 2005.
Griggs, Terry. *Cat's Eye Corner.* Vancouver: Raincoast, 2002.
—. *The Silver Door.* Vancouver: Raincoast, 2004.
Harrison, Troon. *Eye of the Wolf.* Markham: Fitzhenry and Whiteside, 2003.
—. *The Separated: Tales of Terre I.* Weston, Connecticut: Brown Barn, 2006.

—. *The Twilight Box: Tales of Terre II*. Weston, Connecticut: Brown Barn, 2007.
Hughes, Monica. *The Keeper of the Isis Light*. London: Hamish Hamilton, 1980.
—. *The Guardian of Isis*. London: Hamish Hamilton, 1981.
—. *The Isis Pedlar*. London: Hamish Hamilton, 1982.
—. *The Maze*. Toronto: HarperCollins Canada, 2002.
—. *The Isis Trilogy*. Toronto: Tundra Books, 2006.
Johansen, K.V. *Torrie and the Dragon*. Montreal: Roussan, 1997.
—. *The Serpent Bride: Stories From Medieval Danish Ballads*. Saskatoon: Thistledown, 1998.
—. *Torrie and the Pirate-Queen*. Toronto: Annick, 2005.
—. *Torrie and the Firebird*. Toronto: Annick, 2006.
—. *Torrie and the Snake-Prince*. Toronto: Annick, 2007.
Katz, Welwyn Wilton. *Witchery Hill*. New York: Atheneum, 1984.
—. *False Face*. Vancouver: Douglas and McIntyre, 1987.
Kernaghan, Eileen. *Dance of the Snow Dragon*. Saskatoon: Thistledown, 1995.
—. *The Snow Queen*. Saskatoon: Thistledown, 2000.
—. *The Alchemist's Daughter*. Saskatoon: Thistledown, 2004.
Kushner, Donn. *Uncle Jacob's Ghost Story*. Toronto: Macmillan Canada, 1984.
Laurence, Margaret. *Jason's Quest*. Toronto: McClelland and Stewart, 1970.
Leavitt, Martine. *The Dollmage*. Red Deer. Red Deer College Press, 2001.
Loughead, Deb. *Time and Again*. Toronto: Sumach, 2004.
Lunn, Janet. *Double Spell*. Toronto: Peter Martin, 1968.
—. *The Root Cellar*. Toronto: Lester & Orpan Dennys, 1981.
—. *Shadow in Hawthorn Bay*. Toronto: Lester & Orpan Dennys, 1986.
Martini, Clem. *The Mob*. Toronto: Kids Can Press, 2004.
—. *The Plague*. Toronto: Kids Can, 2005.
—. *The Judgment*. Toronto: Kids Can, 2006.
McCurdy, J. Fitzgerald. *The Serpent's Egg*. Ottawa: Saratime Publishing, 2001.
—. *The Burning Crown*. Ottawa: Saratime Publishing, 2002.
—. *The Twisted Blade*. Ottawa: Saratime Publishing, 2003.
—. *The Fire Demons*. Toronto: HarperCollins Canada, 2004.
—. *The Serpent's Egg*. Toronto: HarperCollins Canada. 2005.
McNaughton, Janet. *The Secret Under My Skin*. Toronto: HarperCollins Canada, 2000.
—. *An Earthly Knight*. Toronto: HarperCollins Canada, 2002.
—. *The Raintree Rebellion*. Toronto: HarperTrophy Canada, 2006.
Melling, O.R. *The Druid's Tune*. London: Penguin, 1983.
—. *The Singing Stone*. Toronto: Penguin Canada, 1986.
—. *The Hunter's Moon*. Toronto: HarperCollins Canada, 1993.
—. *The Summer King*. Toronto: Penguin Canada, 1999.
—. *The Light-Bearer's Daughter*. Toronto: Penguin Canada, 2001.
—. *The Chronicles of Faerie*. Toronto: Penguin Canada, 2002.
—. *The Druid's Tune*. Toronto: Penguin Canada, 2003.
—. *The Book of Dreams*. Toronto: Penguin Canada, 2003.
—. *The Singing Stone*. Toronto: Penguin Canada, 2004.
—. *The Golden Book of Faerie*. Toronto: Penguin Canada, 2004.
—. *The Hunter's Moon*. 2nd. Edn. New York: Amulet Books, 2005.
—. *The Summer King*. 2nd. Edn. New York: Amulet Books, 2006.

—. *The Light-Bearer's Daughter*. 2nd Edn. New York: Amulet Books, 2007.
Mills, J.C. *The Sacred Seal*. Toronto: Key Porter Books, 2001.
—. *The Messengers*. Toronto: Key Porter Books, 2002.
—. *The Book of the Sage*. Toronto: Key Porter Books, 2004.
Mullin, Caryl Cude. *A Riddle of Roses*. Toronto: Second Story, 2000.
Nagai-Berthrong, Evelyn, and Anker Odum. *Adventures of the Magic Monkey Along the Silk Roads*. Toronto: Royal Ontario Museum, 1983.
Nicols, Ruth. *A Walk Out of the World*. Don Mills: Longmans Canada, 1969.
—. *The Marrow of the World*. Toronto: Macmillan, 1972.
Oppel, Kenneth. *Silverwing*. Toronto: HarperCollins Canada, 1997.
—. *Sunwing*. Toronto: HarperCollins Canada, 1999.
—. *Firewing*. Toronto: HarperCollins Canada, 2002.
—. *Airborn*. Toronto: HarperCollins Canada, 2004.
—. *Skybreaker*. Toronto: HarperCollins Canada, 2005.
Palmer, Judd. *The Tooth Fairy*. Calgary: Bayeux Arts, 2002.
—. *The Maestro*. Calgary: Bayeax Arts, 2002.
—. *The Wolf King*. Calgary: Bayeax Arts, 2003.
—. *The Sorcerer's Last Words*. Calgary: Bayeax Arts, 2003.
—. *The Giant Killer*. Calgary: Bayeax Arts, 2004.
Pearson, Kit. *A Handful of Time*. Markham: Viking Kestrel, 1987.
Richardson, Bill. *After Hamelin*. Toronto: Annick, 2000.
Richler, Mordecai. *Jacob Two-Two Meets the Hooded Fang*. Toronto: McClelland & Stewart, 1975.
Shields, Carol. *Larry's Party*. Toronto: Random House Canada, 1997.
Slade, Arthur G. *Draugr*. Victoria: Orca Book Publishers, 1997.
—. *The Haunting of Drang Island*. Victoria: Orca Book Publishers, 1998.
—. *The Loki Wolf*. Victoria: Orca Book Publishers, 2000.
Slade, Arthur. *Dust*. Toronto: HarperCollins Canada, 2001.
Smith, Linda. *Wind Shifter*. Saskatoon: Thistledown, 1995.
—. *Sea Change*. Saskatoon: Thistledown, 1999.
—. *The Turning Time*. Saskatoon: Thistledown, 2001.
—. *The Minstrel's Daughter*. Regina: Coteau Books, 2004.
—. *Talisa's Song*. Regina: Coteau, 2005.
Spalding, Andrea. *The Keeper and the Crows*. Victoria: Orca Book Publishers, 2000.
—. *The White Horse Talisman*. Victoria: Orca Book Publishers, 2001.
—. *Dance of the Stones*. Victoria: Orca Book Publishers, 2003.
—. *Heart of the Hill*. Victoria: Orca Book Publishers, 2005.
—. *Behind the Sorcerer's Cloak*. Victoria: Orca Book Publishers, 2006.
Stewart, Sean. *Nobody's Son*. Don Mills: Maxwell Macmillan Canada, 1993.
Tate, Nikki. *Cave of Departure*. Winlaw, BC: Sono Nis Press, 2002.
—. *Jo's Triumph*. Victoria: Orca Book Publishers, 2002.
—. *The Battle for Carnillo*. Winlaw, BC: Sono Nis Press, 2003.
—. *Jo's Journey*. Victoria: Orca Book Publishers, 2006.
Taylor, Cora. *Julie*. Saskatoon: Western Producer Prairie Books, 1985.
—. *The Doll*. Saskatoon: Western Producer Prairie Books, 1987.
—. *Julie's Secret*. Saskatoon: Western Producer Prairie Books, 1991.
—. *Ghost Voyages*. Richmond Hill: Scholastic Canada, 1992.

—. *Ghost Voyages II: The Matthew*. Regina: Coteau Books, 2002.
—. *On Wings of a Dragon*. Markham: Fitzhenry & Whiteside, 2001.
—. *On Wings of Evil*. Markham: Fitzhenry & Whiteside, 2005.
Thornton, Duncan. *Kalifax*. Regina: Coteau, 1999.
—. *Captain Jenny and the Sea of Wonders*. Regina: Coteau, 2001.
—. *The Star-Glass*. Regina: Coteau, 2003.
Tumanov, Vladimir. *Jayden's Rescue*. Toronto: Scholastic Canada, 2002.
Van Belkom, Edo. *Wolf Pack*. Toronto: Tundra Books, 2004.
—. *Lone Wolf*. Toronto: Tundra Books, 2005.

ii. SECONDARY SOURCES

Butcher, Kristin. Review: *The Silver Door*. *CM Magazine* Volume X, Number 20, June 4, 2004.
http://www.umanitoba.ca/outreach/cm/vol10/no20/thesilverdoor.html
Carpenter, Humphrey. *J.R.R. Tolkien: A Biography*. London: Allen and Unwin, 1977.
Carpenter, Humphrey. Ed. *The Letters of J.R.R. Tolkien*. Boston: Houghton Mifflin, 1981.
—. *The Inklings: C.S. Lewis, J.R.R. Tolkien, Charles Williams, and Their Friends*. (1978). London: HarperCollins, 1997.
Carpenter, Humphrey, and Mari Prichard. *The Oxford Companion to Children's Literature*. Oxford: Oxford UP, 1984.
Coleridge, Samuel Taylor. *Biographia Literaria*. 2 Vols. 2nd Edn. New York: George P. Putnam, 1848.
Egoff, Sheila. *The Republic of Childhood: A Critical Guide to Canadian Children's Literature in English*. Toronto: Oxford UP, 1967.
Egoff, Sheila A. *Worlds Within: Children's Fantasy from the Middle Ages to Today*. Chicago: American Library Association, 1988.
Egoff, Sheila, and Judith Saltman. *The New Republic of Childhood: A Critical Guide to Canadian Children's Literature in English*. Toronto: Oxford UP, 1990.
Evans, Gwyneth. "'Nothing odd *ever* happens here': landscape in Canadian fantasy". *Canadian Children's Literature* No. 15/16, 1980, pp. 15-30.
Johansen, K.V. *Quests and Kingdoms: A Grown-Up's Guide to Children's Fantasy Literature*. Sackville: Sybertooth, 2005.
Lewis, C.S. *An Experiment in Criticism*. Cambridge: Cambridge UP, 1961.
—. *Studies in Medieval and Renaissance Literature*. Cambridge: Cambridge UP, 1966.
Ketcheson, Ann. Review: *The Serpent's Egg*. *CM Magazine* Volume XII, Number 18, May 12, 2006.
http://www.umanitoba.ca/outreach/cm/vol12/no18/theserpentsegg.html
MacLeod, Susan. "Life as a Parent: The top twenty breakthroughs: How life has changed in the last twenty years". *Today's Parent*, Oct. 2004.
http://www.todaysparent.com/lifeasparent/parenting/article.jsp?content=20040 907_154326_5240&page=1 (accessed July 11, 2005).
McInnes, John A. Ed. *Magic and Make-Believe*. Don Mills: T. Nelson, 1962.

—. Ed. *Mr. Whiskers*. Don Mills: Thomas Nelson & Sons, 1970.
Oxford English Dictionary Online. "manorial". (Draft revision, Sept. 2000, for the New Edition). 2007.
Oxford English Dictionary Online. "sub-creation". (2nd Edn, 1989). 2007.
Payzant, Tony. Review: *Tunnels of Terror: Another Moose Jaw Adventure*. CM *Magazine* Volume VIII Number 14, March 15, 2002.
http://www.umanitoba.ca/outreach/cm/vol8/no14/tunnels.html
Saltman, Judith. *Modern Canadian Children's Books*. Toronto: Oxford UP, 1987.
—. "The development of Canadian fantasy literature for children". *Canadian Children's Literature* No. 82, Vol. 22:2, 1996, pp. 69-79.
Saul, Nigel. General Editor. *The National Trust Historical Atlas of Britain: Prehistoric to Medieval Britain*. Stroud, Gloucestershire: Sutton Publishing, 1994.
Shippey, T.A. *The Road to Middle-earth*. 2nd Edn. London: Grafton, 1992.
Shippey, T.A. *J.R.R. Tolkien: Author of the Century*. London: HarperCollins, 2000.
Tolkien, J.R.R. *The Monsters and the Critics and Other Essays*. London: HarperCollins, 1997.
—. *Beowulf and the Critics*. Ed. Michael D.C. Drout. Tempe, Arizona: Arizona Center for Medieval and Renaissance Studies, 2002.

iii. NON-CANADIAN FICTION[1]

Adams, Richard. *Watership Down*. London: MacMillan, 1972.
Aiken, Joan. *The Wolves of Willoughby Chase*. London: Jonathan Cape, 1962.
—. *The Witch of Clatteringshaws*. New York : Delacorte Press, 2005.
Alexander, Lloyd. *The Book of Three*. New York: Holt, Rinehart & Winston, 1964.
—. *The High King*. New York: Holt, Rinehart & Winston, 1968.
—. *Westmark*. New York: Dell, 1981.
Andersen, Hans Christian. "The Little Mermaid". 1836.
—. "The Snow Queen. 1846.
Barrie, J.M. *Peter and Wendy*. 1911.
Baum, L. Frank. *The Wonderful Wizard of Oz*. 1900.
Bellairs, John. *The Curse of the Blue Figurine*. New York: Scholastic, 1983.
Briggs, K.M. *Hobberdy Dick*. London: Eyre & Spottiswoode, 1955.
Buchan, John. *The Magic Walking Stick*. London: Hodder & Stoughton, 1932.
Carroll, Lewis. *Alice's Adventures in Wonderland*. 1865.
—. *Through the Looking Glass and What Alice Found There*. 1872.
Cherryh, C.J. *Gate of Ivrel*. New York: Daw Books, 1976.

---

[1] Only the date of original publication, rather than complete bibliographic data, is given for older fantasy classics which have been published in many editions over the years. (For novels initially published as serials, the date is for publication in book form.) For more recent books, bibliographic data for first publication is given where possible, in order to place the books in their historical context for comparison to contemporary Canadian works.

Ciddor, Anna. *Runestone*. Sydney NSW: Allen & Unwin, 2002.
—. *Wolfspell*. Sydney NSW: Allen & Unwin, 2003.
—. *Stormriders*. Sydney NSW: Allen & Unwin, 2004.
Cooper, Susan. *Over Sea, Under Stone*. London: Jonathan Cape, 1965/New York: Harcourt, Brace & World, 1965.
—. *The Dark is Rising*. London: Chatto & Windus, 1973/New York: Margaret K. McElderry, 1973.
—. *The Grey King*. London: Chatto & Windus, 1975/New York: Margaret K. McElderry, 1975.
de la Mare, Walter. *The Three Mulla-Mulgars*. London: Duckworth, 1910.
Dean, Pamela. *Tam Lin*. New York: Tor, 1991.
Ende, Michael. *The Neverending Story*. Trans. Ralph Manheim. Garden City, NY: Doubleday, 1983. (*Die Unendliche Geschichte*, 1979).
Farmer, Penelope. *Charlotte Sometimes*. London: Chatto & Windus, 1969.
Gaiman, Neil. *Coraline*. London: Bloomsbury, 2002.
Garner, Alan. *The Weirdstone of Brisingamen*. London: Collins, 1960.
—. *The Moon of Gomrath*. London: Collins, 1963.
Grahame, Kenneth. *The Wind in the Willows*. New York: Charles Scribner's Sons, 1908.
Grimm, Jacob and Wilhelm. *The Complete Fairy Tales of the Brothers Grimm*. Trans. Jack Zipes. New York: Bantam, 1992.
Ibbotson, Eva. *Which Witch?* London: Macmillan, 1979.
—. *The Secret of Platform 13*. London: Macmillan, 1994.
—. *Island of the Aunts*. London: Macmillan, 1999.
Jacques, Brian. *Redwall*. London: Hutchinson, 1986.
Jansson, Tove. *Comet in Moominland*. London: Ernest Benn, 1951. (*Kometjakten*, 1946).
Jones, Diana Wynne. *Wilkins' Tooth*. London: Macmillan, 1973.
—. *The Ogre Downstairs*. London: Macmillan, 1974.
—. *Charmed Life*. London: Macmillan, 1977
—. *Cart and Cwidder*. London: Macmillan, 1975.
—. *Dogsbody*. London: Macmillan, 1975.
—. *Time of the Ghost*. London: Macmillan, 1981.
—. *The Homeward Bounders*. London: Macmillan, 1981.
—. *Archer's Goon*. London: Methuen, 1984.
—. *Fire and Hemlock*. London: Methuen, 1985.
—. *Howl's Moving Castle*. London: Methuen, 1986.
—. *A Tale of Time City*. London: Methuen, 1987.
—. *Hexwood*. London: Methuen, 1993.
—. *The Merlin Conspiracy*. London: HarperCollins, 2003.
—. *The Pinhoe Egg*. London: HarperCollins, 2006.
Juster, Norton. *The Phantom Tollbooth*. New York : Random House, 1961.
Kingsley, Charles. *The Water-Babies: A Fairy-Tale For a Land-Baby*. 1893.
Kipling, Rudyard. *Puck of Pook's Hill*. 1906.
—. *Rewards and Fairies*. 1910.
Lang, Andrew. *The Gold of Fairnilee*. 1888.
—. *The Blue Fairy Book*. 1889.
—. *The Lilac Fairy Book*. 1910.

Lasky, Katherine. *Guardians of Ga'Hoole: The Capture*. New York: Scholastic, 2003.
LeGuin, Ursula K. *A Wizard of Earthsea*. Berkeley: Parnassus Press, 1968.
—. *The Tombs of Atuan*. New York, Atheneum, 1971.
—. *Tales From Earthsea*. New York: Harcourt, 2001.
—. *The Other Wind*. New York: Harcourt, 2001.
L'Engle, Madeleine. *A Wrinkle in Time*. New York: Farrar, Straus, & Giroux, 1962.
Lewis, C.S. *The Lion, The Witch and the Wardrobe*. London: Macmillan, 1950.
—. *The Silver Chair*. London: Macmillan, 1953.
—. *The Magician's Nephew*. London: Macmillan, 1956.
Lively, Penelope. *The Revenge of Samuel Stokes*. London: Heinemann, 1981.
MacDonald, George. *At the Back of the North Wind*. 1871.
—. *The Princess and the Goblin*. 1872.
—. *The Princess and Curdie*. 1883.
Masefield, John. *The Midnight Folk*. London: Heinemann 1927.
—. *The Box of Delights*. London: Heinemann, 1935.
Mayne, William. *A Grass Rope*. London: Oxford University Press, 1957.
—. *Earthfasts*. London: Hamish Hamilton, 1966.
—. *It*. London: Hamish Hamilton, 1977.
McKillip, Patricia A. *Winter Rose*. New York: Ace Books, 1996.
McKinley, Robin. *Beauty*. New York: Pocket Books, 1978.
—. *The Blue Sword*. New York: Greenwillow Books, 1982.
—. *The Hero and the Crown*. New York: Greenwillow Books, 1985.
—. *The Outlaws of Sherwood*. New York: Greenwillow Books, 1988.
—. *Deerskin*. New York: Ace Books, 1993.
—. *Rose Daughter*. New York: Greenwillow Books, 1997.
—. *Spindle's End*. New York: G.P. Putnam's Sons, 2000.
Murphy, Jill. *The Worst Witch*. London: Allison & Busby, 1974.
Nesbit, E. *Five Children and It*. 1902.
—. *The Story of the Amulet*. 1906.
—. *House of Arden*. 1908.
—. *Harding's Luck*. 1909.
—. *Wet Magic*. 1913
Nix, Garth. *The Ragwitch*. New York: Tor, 1994.
—. *Sabriel*. Pymble NSW: HarperCollins Australia, 1995.
—. *Shade's Children*. New York: HarperCollins, 1997.
—. *The Seventh Tower: The Fall*. New York: Scholastic, 2000.
—. *The Keys to the Kingdom: Mister Monday*. New York: Scholastic, 2003.
Norton, Mary. *The Borrowers*. London: Dent, 1952.
Orwell, George. *Animal Farm*. London: Secker & Warburg, 1945.
—. *Nineteen Eighty-Four*. London: Secker & Warburg, 1949.
Pearce, Philippa. *Tom's Midnight Garden*. London: Oxford University Press, 1958.
Pierce, Tamora. *Alanna: The First Adventure*. New York: Atheneum, 1983.
Potter, Beatrix. *The Tale of Peter Rabbit*. (1901). London: Warne & Co., 1902.
Pratchett, Terry. *The Colour of Magic*. London: Colin Smythe, 1983.
—. *Only You Can Save Mankind*. London: Doubleday, 1992.

—. *Johnny and the Bomb*. London: Doubleday, 1996.
—. *The Wee Free Men*. London: Doubleday, 2003.
Pratchett, Terry, Ian Stewart & Jack Cohen. *The Science of Discworld*. London: Ebury, 2000.
Pullman, Philip. *The Golden Compass*. New York: Alfred A. Knopf, 1995. (UK: *His Dark Materials: Northern Lights*.)
—. *I Was a Rat*. New York: Knopf, 1999.
Rowling, J.K. *Harry Potter and the Philosopher's Stone*. London: Bloomsbury, 1997.
Ruskin, John. *The King of the Golden River*. 1851.
Stewart, Mary. *The Crystal Cave*. London: Hodder & Stoughton, 1970.
Sutcliff, Rosemary. *The Eagle of the Ninth*. Oxford: Oxford UP, 1954.
—. *The Lantern Bearers*. Oxford: Oxford UP, 1959.
Takahashi, Rumiko. *Inuyasha* Vol 1. 2nd Edn. Trans. Mari Morimuto. San Fransciso: Viz Media, 2003. (Japanese publication Shogakukan 1997; 1st Eng. Edn. 1998).
Thackeray, William Makepeace. *The Rose and the Ring*. 1855.
Tolkien, J.R.R. *The Hobbit*. London: Allen & Unwin, 1937. 4th Edn. Allen & Unwin, 1978.
—. *The Fellowship of the Rings*. London: Allen & Unwin, 1954.
—. *The Two Towers*. London: Allen & Unwin, 1954.
—. *The Return of the King*. London: Allen & Unwin, 1955.
—. *The Lord of the Rings*. 2nd Edn. London: Allen & Unwin, 1968. Unwin Hymen, 1988.
Trease, Geoffrey. *Cue For Treason*. Oxford: Blackwell, 1940.
Travers, P.L. *Mary Poppins*. New York: Harcourt, 1934.
Uttley, Alison. *A Traveller in Time*. London: Faber & Faber, 1939.
Verne, Jules. *Journey to the Centre of the Earth*. 1864.
—. *From the Earth to the Moon*. 1865.
—. *20,000 Leagues Under the Sea*. 1870.
Wrede, Patricia C. and Caroline Stevermer. *Sorcery and Cecelia*. New York: Ace Books, 1988.
Wrede, Patricia C. *Snow White and Rose Red*. New York: Tor Books, 1989.
—. *Mairelon the Magician*. New York: Tor Books, 1991.
—.*The Magician's Ward*. 1997.
Wrightson, Patricia. *The Ice is Coming*. London : Hutchinson, 1977.
Wu Cheng'en. *Journey to the West*. (Abridged version). Trans. W.J.F. Jenner. Hong Kong: The Commercial Press, 1994. (circa 1570's).
Yolen, Jane. *Briar Rose*. New York: Tor Books, 1992.

INDEX

aboriginal folktales, 71
aboriginals, 10, 16, 23, 42, 55-6
Adams, Richard, 84
adult fantasy, 8, 17, 25, 102, 105, 121, 122
Adventures of the Magic Monkey Along the Silk Road, 85
Aesop, 29
Africa, 51, 84
After Hamelin, 72, 77
Aiken, Joan, 19, 102
Airborn, 119-20
Alanna: The First Adventure, 24, 125
Alchemist's Daughter, The, 78
alchemy, 42, 79
Alexander, Lloyd, 20, 24, 97, 103, 107, 128-29
Alice's Adventures in Wonderland, 15, 27, 29
aliens, 61-64
allegory, 9, 12, 84, 117
alternate history, 102-3
alternate world fantasy, 102-23, 129
alternate worlds, 19, 61, 67, 88, 102, 119, 123
anachronisms, 34, 82, 96, 105
Andersen, Hans Christian, 15, 71
androids, 61
angels, 46, 53, 94, 95
animal fantasy, 24, 84-7, 119, 128
Animal Farm, 84
animals, 16, 24, 57-8, 70, 72, 81, 84, 116, 119, 122
Ann Connor-Brimer Award, 73
anthologies, 121
apocalypse, 61, 65, 67, 114
Archer's Goon, 41
Arthur, King, 61, 78, 106
At the Back of the North Wind, 15
Aurora Award, 58, 71, 104, 105
Australia, 10, 16, 20, 23-4, 61, 80, 83, 129

Baird, Alison, 8, 50-1, 55, 94-5, 101, 122
ballads, 70, 73-4, 76
Barrie, J.M., 15
Bates, Martine, 104, 108
Battle for Carnillo, The, 118
Baum, L. Frank, 15, 88, 103
BBC, 26
Beauty, 70
"Beauty and the Beast", 70
Bedard, Michael, 13, 42
Begamudré, Ven, 115-16
beginning readers, 43, 47, 80, 83, 91, 92, 98, 104
Behind the Sorcerer's Cloak, 47
Bellairs, John, 21, 62
Beowulf, 7, 28-9
Bhutan, 71
Biographia Literaria, 27
Bishop, Mary Harelkin, 35, 39
Blue Fairy Book, The, 15
Blue Girl, The, 52-3
Blue Roan Child, The, 116-18
Blue Sword, The, 24, 103, 125
Blum, Vicki, 90-2, 101, 103
Bone Flute, The, 56
Book of Dreams, The, 53, 55-6
Book of the Sage, The, 47
Book of Three, The, 20, 97, 103, 106
Book of Wirrun, The, 10, 16, 20, 55
book reviews, 25-6, 35
bookstores, 24-26, 83
Borrowers, The, 41, 48
Boston, L.M., 17
Bow, Patricia, 56
Box of Delights, The, 15
"Boy Who Cried Wolf, The", 75
boys, reading habits of, 124
Bradford, Karleen, 104, 107
Briar Rose, 70
Briggs, K.M., 78

Britain, 7-10, 12-5, 19, 21-4, 30, 33, 42, 45-6, 56, 78, 84-5, 89, 103, 106, 115, 126
British Columbia, 14, 16, 58
brownies, 14, 53
Brownies, The, 10, 14-5, 25, 42
Browning, Robert, 72
Buchan, John, 16, 33
Buddhism, 71, 84
Buffie, Margaret, 92-3, 100
bullying, 49, 50, 63, 105
Burning Crown, The, 95
Butala, Sharon, 55
Calvinism, 25
Canadian Children's Literature, 13, 17
"Canlit", 63, 120
Captain Jenny and the Sea of Wonders, 113
Carnegie Medal, 25
Carpenter, Humphrey, 7, 24-5, 44
Carroll, Lewis, 15, 27
Cart and Cwidder, 20, 103
Cat's Eye Corner, 99-100
Cave of Departure, The, 118
CBC, 124
Charmed Life, 19, 88
Cherryh, C.J., 125
"children don't read fantasy", 8, 104
China, 35, 56, 84
Chrestomanci series, 19, 102
Christianity, 71, 78, 94, 116
Chronicles of Faerie, The, 53-55
Chronicles of Narnia, The, 88, 127
Chronicles of Prydain, The, 20, 127
Ciddor, Anna, 80-83
"Cinderella", 70
CLA Book of the Year for Children Award, 16, 18, 21, 22, 23, 85
CLA Young Adult Canadian Book Award, 11, 53, 104
Clark, Catherine Anthony, 14-19, 22, 24, 42
CM Magazine, 25-6, 35
Coleridge, Samuel Taylor, 27
Colour of Magic, The, 103
Comet in Moominland, 103
Cooper, Susan, 41, 45, 128-29

Coraline, 127, 136
Cox, Palmer, 14, 25, 42
Crooked House, The, 104-5
Crystal Cave, The, 78
Cue For Treason, 79
Curse of the Blue Figurine, The, 62
cyborgs, 61
Czerneda, Julie E., 120-23
Daily Telegraph newspaper, 26
Dalemark Quartet, 20
Dance of the Snow Dragon, 71
Dance of the Stones, 46
Dark is Rising, The, 41, 127
de la Mare, Walter, 15, 84
de Lint, Charles, 30, 52, 55, 59, 70, 122
Dean, Pamela, 73
Deerskin, 70
demons, 32, 51, 56, 62-3, 95, 97
Denmark, 2, 71, 78
Dickinson, Peter, 21
didactic literature, 7, 14, 16, 24-5, 29, 30, 50, 99, 127-28
Dirt Eaters, The, 65
Discworld, 103
Dogsbody, 41
Doll, The, 33, 109
Dollmage, 107
dolls, 21, 33, 108
Double Spell, 21-3, 33
Dragonfire, 107
dragons, 7, 56, 61, 72-3, 84, 107, 110, 121
Dragon's Egg, The, 8, 50
Dragon's Tapestry, The, 108
Draugr, 43
Dreaming Place, The, 52
druids, 11, 94-5
Druid's Tune, The, 8, 11, 53
dual-world fantasy, 70, 88-101, 103-4, 122, 125, 129
Duncan, Dave, 30, 104, 122
Dust, 62, 120
dwarves, 15, 98, 103
Eagle of the Ninth, The, 114
Earthfasts, 19, 22
Earthly Knight, An, 73-4, 76, 78

"East of the Sun, West of the Moon", 29
eddas, 80
Egoff, Sheila, 12-16, 21-25, 62
elves, 90, 95-6, 98, 114
Ende, Michael, 50, 88
England, 12, 19, 32, 45, 47, 78, 102
epic, 10-11, 19, 48, 84, 86, 93, 98
Evans, Gwyneth, 17, 19
Experiment in Criticism, An, 27
extra-terrestrials. See aliens
Eye of the Wolf, 60-1, 68
fables, 11, 29
fairies, 11-12, 14-15, 28, 41-42, 48, 53-6, 70, 73-4, 90, 93-5, 104, 106
Fairy Books, 15, 70-71
fairy-tales, 11-12, 15, 28-9, 70-3, 75-76, 83, 104, 110, 116
family history, 11, 21, 23, 33, 39, 128
Fantastic Companions, 121
fantasy readers, 27, 42, 92, 101, 121-22, 125
fantasy, characteristics of, 10-14, 17-23, 26-8, 48, 59, 64, 69, 85, 115, 122
fantasy, functions of, 9, 28-9, 69, 76, 89, 125
fantasy, qualities of Canadian, 7-14, 17, 24-5, 29-30, 39, 83, 87, 100-01, 104, 111, 120, 123, 126-9
Farmer, Penelope, 23
Fast, A.D., 36, 38-9
Feather and Bone: The Crow Chronicles, 86
feminism, 20, 125
feudalism, 36
Finder, The, 93
Findlay, Jamieson, 116-17, 122-23
Finland, 71
Fire and Hemlock, 73
Fire Demons, The, 63
Firewing, 85-6
Five Children and It, 15, 41, 127
Fixed, 67-8
Flux, 67-8
folklore, 11, 14, 41-5, 52, 54-6, 71, 78, 80, 106
folklorists, 80

folktales, 12, 15, 57, 70-1, 76-8, 83-4
Foon, Dennis, 65-7, 69
Freewalker, 65-6
French-Canadian folktales, 71
Freyan Trilogy, The, 111-12
From the Earth to the Moon, 60
Garner, Alan, 19, 41, 45
Gate of Ivrel, 125
Gathering of Unicorns, A, 90
gender imbalance, 124
Geoffrey of Monmouth, 78
Germany, 24, 56
Ghost Voyages, 33, 109
Ghost Voyages II: The Matthew, 33, 109
ghosts, 11, 20-2, 34, 38-9, 42, 52, 68, 75, 78-9
"Giant, The", 55
giants, 55, 70, 75, 96
Gilgamesh, The Epic of, 29
goblins, 56, 113
goddesses, 20-21, 85, 121
gods, 54-56, 68, 85, 93-4
Gold of Fairnilee, The, 70, 73, 78
Golden Book of Faerie, The, 53
Golden Compass, The, 25
Golden Pine Cone, The, 16
Goobie, Beth, 67-69
Goodfellow Chronicles, The, 47-48
Governor-General's Award, 42, 62, 75, 120
Grahame, Kenneth, 15, 84
Grass Rope, A, 19
Greenwood, Ed, 121
Grey King, The, 41
Griggs, Terry, 26, 99-100
Grimm, Jakob and Wilhelm, 15
Guardians of Ga'Hoole, 87
Handful of Time, A, 23, 33
Harding's Luck, 23
Harp of the Grey Rose, The, 52
Harrison, Troon, 60, 68
Harry Potter, 8, 26, 42
Harry Potter and the Philosopher's Stone, 8, 42
Haunting of Drang Island, The, 43
Heart of the Hill, 47
Hero and the Crown, The, 24, 125

Hexwood, 61
Hidden Land, The, 55
Hidden World, The, 51, 94
High King, The, 20
Hinduism, 56
historical fantasy, 70, 73, 78-83, 128
historical fiction, 7, 11, 22, 29, 32-3, 39, 43, 46-7, 73-4, 78, 80, 82, 107, 114, 118, 128
Hobberdy Dick, 78
Hobbit, The, 15, 44, 103, 127
hobgoblins, 78
Holocaust, the, 70
Homeward Bounders, The, 61, 88
horror, 8, 58
House of Arden, 23, 31
Howl's Moving Castle, 24, 88
Hughes, Monica, 48
Hunter's Moon, The, 53, 56
I Was a Rat!, 70
Ibbotson, Eva, 21, 42
Ice Is Coming, The, 20
Iceland, 43
Iliad, The, 29
immigration, 12, 55, 78
Inuit, 56
Inuyasha, 32
Ireland, 11, 53-6, 93, 94
Isis Trilogy, The, 48, 132
Island of the Aunts, 42
It, 19
J.R.R. Tolkien: Author of the Century, 26
Jack the Giant-Killer, 70
"Jack the Giant-Killer", 75
Jacob Two-Two Meets the Hooded Fang, 11
Jacques, Brian, 24, 85, 87, 126
Jansson, Tove, 103
Japan, 32
Jason's Quest, 84
Jayden's Rescue, 99
Johnny and the Bomb, 32
Jones, Diana Wynne, 19-20, 23-4, 41, 61, 73, 88, 101-03, 126, 129
Jo's Journey, 118
Jo's Triumph, 118
Journey to the Centre of the Earth, 61

Journey to the West, 84
Judgment, The, 87
Julie, 14, 23, 33, 42, 109
Julie's Secret, 109
Juster, Norton, 99
Kalifax, 113
Katz, Welwyn Wilton, 11, 13, 42
Keeper and the Crows, The, 43-5
Keeper's Shadow, The, 66
Kernaghan, Eileen, 71-2, 78-9
Keys to the Kingdom, The, 89, 127
Kierans, Genevieve, 122
King of the Golden River, The, 15
King's Blades, 105
King's Daggers, The, 104-05
Kingsley, Charles, 15
Kipling, Rudyard, 15, 17, 32-4
Kushner, Donn, 11
Lake of Gold, 16, 33
Land Without Unicorns, The, 90
landscape, 10, 16, 19, 20, 22, 33, 45, 55, 110, 114-15
Lang, Andrew, 15, 70-71, 73, 78
Lantern Bearers, The, 114
Larry's Party, 124
Lasky, Katherine, 87
Laurence, Margaret, 84, 87
Layamon's *Brut*, 28
Leavitt, Martine, 104, 108
legends, 10-11, 19, 23, 41, 53-4, 70-2, 78, 94-5, 114-16
LeGuin, Ursula K., 20
L'Engle, Madeleine, 20, 46
Letters of J.R.R. Tolkien, The, 44
Lewis, C.S., 15, 17, 27-8, 88, 103, 113
libraries, 8-9, 53, 83, 98, 104, 114, 127
light fantasy, 11
Light-Bearer's Daughter, The, 53
Lilac Fairy Book, The, 15
Lion, the Witch and the Wardrobe, The, 88, 103
literacy, 127
literary belief, 13, 28, 52, 64, 77, 96, 98, 100, 109, 112, 120
literary criticism, 13, 24-7, 63, 120, 124
"Little Mermaid, The", 15

Lively, Penelope, 21, 41
Lives of Christopher Chant, The, 127
Loki Wolf, The, 43, 59
Lone Wolf, 59
Long Traverse, The. See: *Lake of Gold*
Longlight Legacy, The, 65-7
Looney Tunes, 36
Lord of the Rings, The, 26-7, 44, 103, 125
Loughead, Deb, 38
Loup Garou, 56
Lunn, Janet, 14, 21-4, 33, 55, 78
Mabinogion, 20
MacDonald, George, 15, 103
Maestro, The, 75
magazines, children's, 15
magic, 8, 11, 13, 16, 19, 22, 29, 31-4, 36, 38-42, 45, 47, 49, 55, 61-4, 71, 76, 78, 80-4, 88, 90-2, 102-116
Magic and Make Believe, 127
Magic Walking Stick, The, 16
magicians, 102, 111-12
Magician's Nephew, The, 113
Magician's Ward, The, 102
Mairelon the Magician, 102
manga, 32
manorialism, 36
Marrow of the World, The, 18, 89
Martini, Clem, 86-7
Mary Poppins, 15
Masefield, John, 15, 17
Mayne, William, 19, 23
Maze, The, 48-50
McCurdy, J. Fitzgerald, 25, 63-4, 95
McKillip, Patricia A., 73
McKinley, Robin, 24, 70, 103, 125
McNaughton, Janet, 61, 73-4, 78
Melling, O.R., 8, 11, 13, 30, 53-6, 59
Merlin, 61, 78
Merlin Conspiracy, The, 89
Mermaid Secret, The, 92
mermaids, 92
Messengers, The, 47
Middle-earth, 103
Midnight Folk, The, 15, 127
Mills, J.C., 47
Minstrel's Daughter, The, 112
Mithras, 65

Mob, The, 86
Modern Canadian Children's Books, 10
Mole Wars, The, 63
Monsters and the Critics and Other Essays, The, 13, 28
Moon of Gomrath, The, 19, 41
morality, 9-10, 25, 29, 117
Morte Darthur, The, 28
Mr. Whiskers, 127
Mullin, Caryl Cude, 106
multiple worlds, 61, 88
Murphy, Jill, 42
mystery novels, 23, 63
Mystery of the Medieval Coin, The, 36, 38-9
myth, 10, 19, 41, 43, 53-4, 78
mythologies, aboriginal, 10, 52, 55-6
mythology, 12, 16, 22, 55-6, 86-7, 94-95, 114
mythology, Celtic, 52, 55, 94-5
mythology, Norse, 43, 71, 80, 95
myths, 10, 42, 70, 78, 93
Nagai-Bertrong, Evelyn, 84
National Trust Historical Atlas of Britain: Prehistoric to Medieval Britain, The, 36
nationalism, 25
nature stories, 7
Nesbit, E., 15, 17, 19, 23, 31, 36, 41, 49
Neverending Story, The, 50, 88
New Republic of Childhood, 12
Newbery Honor books, 21, 24, 41
Newbery Medal, 20, 24, 41
Newfoundland, 73, 94
Newfoundland and Labrador Book Award, 73
Nichols, Ruth, 14, 17-19, 24, 89, 100, 104
Nineteen Eighty-Four, 68
Nix, Garth, 61, 83, 89, 103-04, 126, 129
Nobody's Son, 104
North America, 25, 67, 82, 112
Northern Frights, 43, 55, 62
Northern Lights. See: *The Golden Compass*

143

North-West Passage, 113
Norton, Mary, 41, 48, 50
Norway, 80
occult, 8
Odum, Anker, 84
"Offering of Trust", 121
Ogre Downstairs, The, 41
Old English, 44
"On Fairy-Stories", 13, 28
On Wings of a Dragon, 109-10
On Wings of Evil, 110
Only You Can Save Mankind, 127, 137
Oppel, Kenneth, 30, 85-7, 119, 122
Orwell, George, 84
Other Wind, The, 20
Otherworld, 52, 56-7, 116
Our Canadian Girl series, 33
Outlaws of Sherwood, The, 70
Over Sea, Under Stone, 41
Oxford Companion to Children's Literature, The, 7, 24
Oxford English Dictionary, 10, 37, 102
Palmer, Judd, 14, 25, 74, 76-7
Paniccia, Jane, 121
parallel worlds. *See* alternate worlds
paranormal, 8, 23, 59, 62, 67, 92, 109
passive plots, 125
passivity of heroes, 125
Pearce, A. Philippa, 22-3, 31
Pearson, Kit, 14, 23, 33
Peter and Wendy, 15
Peter Pan, 15
Phantom Queen, The, 115
Phantom Tollbooth, The, 99
picture books, 2, 47, 70-2, 76, 111
Pied Piper, the, 72
Pierce, Tamora, 24, 125
Pinhoe Egg, The, 127, 136
Plague, The, 87
plays, 65, 76, 86
poetry, 27, 38, 44, 71, 115
Potter, Beatrix, 84
Pratchett, Terry, 32, 103, 126
"Prayer of Salt and Sand, A", 121
Preposterous Fables for Unusual Children, 74-6

Prichard, Mari, 24-5
primary world, 10, 13, 41-2, 52, 59, 62-3, 88, 101-4, 107, 112, 128-29
Princess and Curdie, The, 15
Princess and the Goblin, The, 15, 103, 127
problem novels, 18, 25, 36, 67
Promise of the Unicorn, The, 90
psychic powers, 11, 14, 23, 62
publishers, 8, 59, 62, 105, 124, 127
publishers, Canadian, 8, 47, 80, 82, 104, 107, 123-24
Puck of Pook's Hill, 15, 32-34
Pullman, Philip, 25, 70
puns, 100
puppets, 76
Québec, 14, 16, 56
Quests and Kingdoms, 2, 6, 30
Ragwitch, The, 127, 137
Raintree Rebellion, The, 61
Ransome, Arthur, 128
reader (textbook), 127
readers, 128
reading difficulties, 82, 91, 127
"realism of content", 28
"realism of presentation", 27
Realms of Wonder, 120, 122, 129
Redwall, 24-5, 85, 87
Redwork, 42
reincarnation, 11, 32, 50-1
related worlds, 19, 102
religion, 21, 25, 36, 63, 65, 68, 79, 85, 105, 109, 116, 121
Republic of Childhood, The, 12-13
Revenge of Samuel Stokes, The, 41
Rewards and Fairies, 15, 32
Richardson, Bill, 72
Riddle of Roses, A, 106
Riddle of the Wren, The, 52
riddles, 44
Road to Middle-earth, The, 44
Robin Hood, 70
Rogers, Stan, 55
romance, 33, 115
romance (love stories), 8, 23
Romances, medieval, 104
Root Cellar, The, 21, 23, 33
Rose and the Ring, The, 15

Rose Daughter, 70
Rowling, J.K., 8, 42, 129
Runestone, 80-2
Ruskin, John, 15
Russia, 116
Sabriel, 103
Sacred Seal, The, 47
sagas, 43, 80
Saltman, Judith, 10-14, 24-5, 62
Saskatchewan, 62, 93
Saskatchewan Book Award, 62
Scandinavia, 24, 71-3, 80
school stories, 27, 83, 124
schools, 9, 50-2, 83, 98, 104, 127
science, 31, 60-62, 68, 71, 119
science fiction, 11, 31, 48, 52, 60-2, 65, 69, 73, 104, 120, 122, 125, 128
Science of Discworld, The, 103
Scotland, 14, 22, 42, 70, 73, 78
Sea Change, 111
second sight, 22, 42, 78-9, 94
Second World War, 32, 47, 61, 94
secondary world fantasy, 8, 10-11, 20, 24, 42, 52, 59, 73, 85, 88, 90, 101-125
secondary worlds, 10-14, 18, 24, 28, 59, 73, 85, 88, 90, 101-25, 129
Secret of Platform 13, The, 42
Secret Under My Skin, The, 61
Seeker, The, 93
Separated, The, 60
Serpent Bride, The, 78
Serpent's Egg, The, 25, 64, 95-6, 98
"Seven Ravens, The", 29
Seventh Tower, The, 83, 103-04, 127
Shade's Children, 61
Shadow in Hawthorn Bay, 22, 55, 78
Shadow Unicorn, The, 90
Shakespeare, William, 28, 79
shamanism, 50-1, 56, 71, 115
Shields, Carol, 124
Shippey, T.A., 26, 44
short stories, 32, 52, 83, 115, 120
Silver Birch Award, 58
Silver Chair, The, 106
Silver Door, The, 26, 99
Silvercloak, 104-05
Silverwing, 85

Singing Stone, The, 53
Sir Stalwart, 104
Skybreaker, 120
Slade, Arthur G., 43, 55, 62, 120
slavery, 57, 74, 81-82, 90-91, 100, 110
Smith, Linda, 104, 111-12
Snow Queen, The, 71, 76
"Snow Queen, The", 15
"Snow White", 71
Snow White and Rose Red, 70
Solomon and Saturn II, 44
"Sorcerer's Apprentice, The", 75
sorcerers, 47, 75, 99
Sorcerer's Last Words, The, 75
sorceresses, 71
Sorcery and Cecelia, 102
Spalding, Andrea, 43-6
Spear of Longinus, 94
speculative fantasy, 61, 69, 128
speculative fiction, 48, 58, 60-61, 64, 69-71, 85, 124
Spindle's End, 70
spirits, 16, 22, 45, 50, 53, 56, 106, 115-16
sports stories, 83, 124
St. Nicholas (magazine), 15
Star-Glass, The, 113-14
Stevermer, Caroline, 102
Stewart, Mary, 78
Stewart, Sean, 104
Stone of the Stars, The, 50
Stormriders, 82
Story of the Amulet, The, 23, 31, 49
Studies in Medieval and Renaissance Literature, 28
sub-creation, 10, 13-14, 102
sub-creator, 13, 28
Summer King, The, 53-6
Summer of Magic Quartet, The, 45-7
Summoned to Destiny, 120
Sumner-Smith, Karina, 121
Sun Horse, The, 16
Sunwing, 85
supernatural, 8, 10-11, 16, 19, 20-3, 27, 41-2, 50, 52, 55-61, 68, 78, 114, 126
"suspension of disbelief", 27-8
Sutcliff, Rosemary, 114, 128

145

Táin bó Cuailnge, 11
Takahashi, Rumiko, 32
Tale of Peter Rabbit, The, 84
Tale of Time City, A, 61
Tales From Earthsea, 20
Tales of Terre, 60
Tales of Three Lands, 112
Talisa's Song, 112
Tam Lin, 73
"Tam Lin", 73
Tate, Nikki, 118
Taylor, Cora, 14, 23, 33-4, 39, 42, 109, 122
technology, 60-6, 68, 82, 105, 119
television, 29, 38, 122
Thackeray, William Makepeace, 15
The Brownies: Their Book, 15
Thornton, Duncan, 113-15, 122
Three Mulla-Mulgars, The, 15, 84, 87
Three Royal Monkeys, The. See: *Three Mulla-Mulgars, The*
Through the Looking-Glass, 15, 27
Tibet, 71
Time and Again, 38-9
Time of the Ghost, 20, 22, 41
time-travel, 9-10, 13-14, 16, 19-23, 29, 31-40, 82, 109, 128
Today's Parent Magazine, 8
Tolkien, J.R.R., 7, 10, 13, 15, 17, 19, 28, 44, 102-04, 114
Tombs of Atuan, The, 21
Tom's Midnight Garden, 22, 31, 36
Tooth Fairy, The, 74
Torrie and the Dragon, 104
Torrie and the Firebird, 104
Torrie and the Pirate-Queen, 104
Torrie and the Snake-Prince, 104
Traveller in Time, A, 22, 31, 36
Travers, P.L., 15
Trease, Geoffrey, 79
trolls, 56, 72, 90
Tumanov, Vladimir, 99
Tunnels of Terror, 35
Tunnels of Time, 35
Tunnels of Treachery, 35
Tunnels of Tyranny, 35
Turning Time, The, 111
Turtledove, Harry, 102

20,000 Leagues Under the Sea, 60
Twilight Box, The, 60
Twin Spell, 21
Twisted Blade, The, 95-6
Uncle Jacob's Ghost Story, 12
unicorns, 90
United States, The, 7-9, 12-15, 17, 19-21, 24-5, 30, 43, 47, 50, 53, 87, 89, 104, 120, 126
Uttley, Alison, 22-3, 31
van Belkom, Edo, 58-9
Verne, Jules, 60-1
Viking Magic, 80-83
Vikings, 80, 94
Waifs and Strays, 52
Wales, 20, 94
Walk Out of the World, A, 17-18, 89, 100
Warding of Willowmere, The, 51
Watcher, The, 92
Water-Babies, The, 15
Watership Down, 84
Wee Free Men, The, 103
Weirdstone of Brisingamen, The, 19, 41, 127
werewolves, 43, 52, 56, 58-9
West of January, 105
West, Michelle, 121
Westmark, 24, 103
Wet Magic, 15
Which Witch?, 42
Whisperings of Magic, 107
White Horse Talisman, The, 45-6
Wide Awake, 15
wilderness, 14, 42, 80, 109, 114
Wilkins' Tooth, 19
Willowmere Chronicles, The, 50-1, 94
Wind in the Willows, The, 15, 84, 87
Wind Shifter, 111
Windling, Terri, 70, 73
Winter Rose, 73
Wish Upon a Unicorn, 90
Witchery Hill, 11
witches, 12, 18, 42, 50-1
Witches of Willowmere, The, 50, 59
Wizard of Earthsea, A, 20
wizards, 41, 63, 78, 102-03, 111
Wolf King, The, 75

Wolf Moon, 52
Wolf Pack, 58-9
Wolfspell, 80-2
Wolves Chronicles, 19, 102
Wolves of Willoughby Chase, The, 19
Wolves of Woden, The, 94-5
Wonderful Wizard of Oz, The, 15, 88
Woozles Bookstore, 8, 24

Wordsworth, William, 28
Worlds Within, 14-17, 21, 23, 30
Worst Witch, The, 42
Wrede, Patricia C., 70, 102
Wrightson, Patricia, 10, 16, 20, 23, 55
Wrinkle in Time, A, 20, 46
Wyrd of Willowmere, 51
Yolen, Jane, 70

Also published by Sybertooth

Nominated for the 2006 Harvey Darton Award
QUESTS AND KINGDOMS
A Grown-Up's Guide to Children's Fantasy Literature
By K.V. Johansen

Quests and Kingdoms provides a basis from which an adult unfamiliar with the genre of children's fantasy literature may explore it. *Quests* is an historical survey for the interested general reader, which will be of great practical value to library and education professionals as well. Though the aim is to give adults concerned with bringing children (or teens) and books together a familiarity with the children's fantasy genre and its history, for those who already know and love the classics of children's fantasy *Quests* will be an introduction to works and authors they may have missed.

Taking a chronological approach, *Quests* begins with the fairy-tale collections of d'Aulnoy, Perrault, and the Grimms and works its way up to the novels of J.K. Rowling and Garth Nix, covering over three centuries of fantasy read by children. The lives of 95 authors are looked at and placed in historical context, while their works are introduced through both synopses and analysis. *Quests* also includes chapters on Tolkien, retellings of traditional stories, and King Arthur and Robin Hood. More than 500 works are discussed, and the thorough index makes the book a practical reference resource as well as a history and an introduction to the best in the genre.

Critical **Praise for** *Quests and Kingdoms*

"....exceptionally well written and recommended for its relevance for teachers and or parents..." - *Midwest Book Review March 2006*

"...this is not only a fine reference tool but a finely-written book...This is undoubtedly a seminal work guaranteed to stimulate discussion on children's literature..." - *Books in Canada Jan/Feb 2006*

"...a fascinating overview of children's fantasy literature... This is a must-dip-into reference book for fantasy lovers but would prove useful to those who know little about the genre and are needing to recommend fantasy writers to both children and adults. It could also prove useful to older pupils who are studying fantasy in their English courses." - *School Librarian journal, V.54, №4, Winter 2006*

"This is a book that does exactly what it says on the tin – and then more...Tolkien is seen as so pivotal in the development of the genre that he gets a thoughtful and well researched chapter all to himself...a helpful guide to content... Her book could be a real help to the adults seeking to guide [children] into this marvellous world." - *Amon Hen (Bulletin of the Tolkien Society), Issue 196*

"What truly amazes, though, is Johansen's reliability and depth of knowledge ...and her accuracy with facts...The sheer volume of knowledge on display here could earn Johansen honors for scholarship. This is a truly useful reference book..." - *Mythprint (Bulletin of the Mythopoeic Society) Nov. 2005*

"In an engaging and highly readable style, Johansen's enthusiasm and knowledge for her subject captivates her reader... Quests and Kingdoms is an informed and informative work highly recommended for reader's advisory, teachers of language arts and fantasy collections." - *CM Magazine Vol. XII No. 2, Sept. 16 2000*

"I can think across the years of Marcus Crouch and Sheila Egoff, Neil Philip and Colin Manlove, Jack Zipes and Humphrey Carpenter, and J.R.R. Tolkien himself ... all of whom have written interestingly and well about fantasy ... Johansen's Quests and Kingdoms is a welcome tradition to this critical tradition."

and,

"Collection builders in a public or school library will find this a useful checklist of what should be there (or what, if it's not there, is not there for very sound reasons). ... for new readers this will excite and identify things to read, and for readers familiar with the field, it will challenge, occasionally irritate, and encourage re-reading." - *Children's Books History Society Newsletter No. 83, Dec. 2005*

"...a valuable reference resource to librarians, education professionals and graduate students in the field of children's and adolescent literature."
- *Resource Links, Volume 11 Number 2, December 2005*

"a lively, thoughtful read, and a useful reference volume" - *Terri Windling*

"Here is a magical thing, a reference book with a heart and soul. Brimming over with ideas, as well as facts and figures, the writing is elegant and the author's enthusiasm contagious. Here, too, a noble defence of fantasy and its literary value." - *O.R. Melling*

"Johansen brings a scholar's erudition and a child's delight to the field of children's fantasy. Her thoughtful survey elevates fantasy from guilty pleasure to moral education, and reveals it to be not a recent marketing-driven fad, but an ancient and unbreakable strand of human creativity. If you know nothing about the genre, this book will turn you into an aficionado; if you think you've read everything, you'll find new gems here, and old ones glowing with a new light. For teachers, parents, anyone who wants to uncover the wonder of reading, Quests and Kingdoms is a pirate's treasure map." - *Tristanne J. Connolly, St. Jerome's University*

462pp • $30.00 (US) • £20.00 (UK) • Trade paperback
ISBN-10: 0968802443 • **ISBN-13:** 9780968802441

Also published by Sybertooth
www.sybertooth.ca

The Canvas Barricade

In print for the first time, Donald Jack's comedy *The Canvas Barricade* was the first Canadian play performed on the main stage of the Stratford Festival (1961).

Misty Woodenbridge, a painter, has rejected the materialism of modern society for life in a tent by the Ottawa River, where he lives as carefree as the fabled grasshopper, eating stolen apples and painting masterpieces. But as summer draws to an end, reality rears its ugly head, and Misty must choose between starving in his tent and moving to the city with his fiancée. Meanwhile, his in-laws-to-be smell a cash cow when a mysterious art buyer begins snapping up Misty's work – and naturally they keep the money. Out of kind consideration for Misty's artistic ideals, of course...

ISBN-10: 0968802494 • **ISBN-13:** 9780968802496
Trade paperback, published 2007
$16.00 (US) • £11.00 (UK) • $18.00 (Can)

Love on the Marsh
By Douglas Lochhead

Internationally-acclaimed poet Douglas Lochhead has been, for over a quarter century, the voice of the Tantramar Marshes. His latest work, *Love on the Marsh*, gives an intimate portrait of the relationship between two lovers set against the unique landscape that Lochhead knows so well.

ISBN-13: 9780973950533
Trade paperback, published 2008

www.ingramcontent.com/pod-product-compliance
Lightning Source LLC
Chambersburg PA
CBHW032051150426
43194CB00006B/488